AUTUMN

An anthology for
the changing seasons

Edited by Melissa Harrison

T0347677

Elliott&Thompson

First published 2016 by
Elliott and Thompson Limited
2 John Street, London WC1N 2ES
www.eandtbooks.com

ISBN: 978-1-78396-248-8

Commissioning editor: Jennie Condell
Series research: Brónagh Woods

9 8 7

A catalogue record for this book is available from
the British Library.

Printed by CPI Group (UK) Ltd, Croydon, CR0 4YY

MIX
Paper | Supporting
responsible forestry
FSC® C171272

CONTENTS

INTRODUCTION

I have always loved autumn. At primary school I learned Keats' famous poem by heart; later, I dreamed of being at university and spending Michaelmas term walking through drifts of russet leaves, sunk in romantic thoughts. Again and again I hear from friends that it is their favourite of all the four seasons; that somehow it makes tangible a suite of emotions – wistfulness, nostalgia, a comfortable kind of melancholy – that are, at other times of the year, just out of reach.

It's hardly surprising. After all, autumn is the natural world's gentle *memento mori*; it's when the year's cycle begins to slow as spring's generative energy and summer's riotous fruition at last start to fail, prompted by shorter days, falling temperatures and the need shared by so many living things for a period of quietude and senescence.

Although not all. Autumn is a busy time for saprophytes: fungi, mould and all the million detritivores whose job it is to recycle organic matter so that it may be used again. To me, the process of decay is about life, not death, the year's spent growth giving rise to the very earth that will propel the following spring. Autumn is a time of new beginnings, too.

And there's no rest in the avian world as the second of the year's great migrations gets underway. Our summer visitors, like the hirundines, the ospreys and many of the warblers head south, and instead we welcome great flocks of wildfowl and thrushes from the north, here to escape colder climes. Passage migrants, too, take advantage of our isles to rest and refuel and keep the hardcore birders busy. Autumn is not a mellow season for all.

It may yet be fruitful, though. In recent years we've begun to rediscover Britain's rich history of local apple varieties, and many villages now celebrate them in October through the relatively new initiative of Apple Day. And although we may be tied far less to the seasons now when it comes to shop-bought food, going blackberrying remains a pleasure that can only be enjoyed at a certain time of year.

Autumn in our temperate region is still a season of mists – and of other atmospheric phenomena, too: equinoctial gales, like the great storm of 1987; the first ground frosts; gossamer spiderwebs at daybreak, hung with sparkling dew. The nights cool, and lengthen; summer, if we've had one, slowly falls behind us. Festivals like Diwali, Halloween and Bonfire Night light up in different ways the gathering dark.

When I went to university I found myself too busy in Michaelmas term to drift around outdoors thinking deep thoughts. But in the years since then I haven't lost my love of autumn – although I've come to appreciate the other seasons, too. There's something so beguiling about the blazing leaves and the rich smell of rot, and the start of a new phase in the circling year.

Melissa Harrison, Autumn 2016

I n the edges of days, in the confluence of tides, in the unclear lapping and lap-backing of the between-seasons is autumn. It can be obvious, a salute of blazing foliage, or disguised, slipping in behind distractions. In the south, the summer of St Martin ends in November, the brightest summer of all, its colours luminous under the Mediterranean blue, which changes, unblazes, dies down from August glare to soft September. *'My favourite month!'* I think, in Septembers like that, forgetting that in July it was all going too quickly and that summer should always be wished for ever. But autumn has a summer and a winter. As I fear the latter a little, I love the former much. You find reflections of both at other times of year. Still spring days when the smoke also rises straight can have a little of autumn in them, the trees in half-colours, the blossom yet to break. Stars at evening seen through near-bare boughs could belong to either season.

I was taught as a child that you find you are ready for each earth tide when it comes. With the years, and with moving from the south to the north, I have learned how age dreads winter, which seems to last longer every time – and actually is longer where I live now. The yellow leaves of the lime trees, desiccated in August and dead in the gutters, always gave me pause in Verona. So soon?

In Palermo we swam until November then put on scarves. In Yorkshire we watch the miracles of the trees across the valley, their colours playing like notes across a keyboard, slowly. The hill opposite our windows is close and covered in

1

a complete wood: alders by the beck, and above them sycamore, pine, birch, ash, oak and beech. We observe them
pulsing through the spectrum in almost bemused delight until
the rain thickens the windows and darkness falls until March.
And then autumn is motorway rain and the dirty courts of
service stations, greys and greases and the smeared crimson
brake lights streaming into junctions, and days that seem to
shut themselves down, disgusted and forgettable.

The names of the northern towns then seem written in
heavy autumnal syllables and rain-dark stone. Warrington,
Salford, Preston, where the equinoctial skies press down. You
wish you were anywhere else. Autumn in New York. Autumn
in Rome, Paris, London: the great cities might be made for the
season, their towers of lights shining for longer as the months
roll darker, and in the cooling mornings the sweet and smoky
smells. In one of those offices I once set radio listeners a writing
competition: winter without clichés. Autumn would have been
much harder.

'Even as a schoolboy I loved John Keats's ode "To Autumn"
for being an ark of the covenant between language and sensation,' Seamus Heaney wrote. It is the time of richest sensation:
the sights and the smells, obviously, and the way its daily varying temperature makes the skin hypersensitive; and then there
are the sounds – rain, wind, dead leaves; and then its harvest of
tastes, from traffic fog to cold clear days. It makes writers of the
most pen-averse of us, because we have a need to turn sensation
into language. In its brightness, its startling quality, its beauty
and its inevitable slide to darkness, it is the season that most
resembles human life. The first moment you can remember
kicking up leaves is probably fairly contiguous with your first

apprehension of death. All humans are in the autumn of their days – that's life, and the other.

To the novelist, autumn offers a believable, dramatic, enticing setting: the trick of fiction is to make-believe, and autumn is the story season, a time of migration, equinox, transformation and incident, the things of which fiction is made. And obviously you want stuff to happen: it suggests adversity and change, great boons to any plot. Dickens was a great fan, beginning *Our Mutual Friend* and *Bleak House* in London autumns. Angela Carter starts *The Magic Toyshop* thus: 'October, crisp, misty, golden October, when the light is sweet and heavy. They stood on the step and waited for the taxi with black bands on their arms and suitcases in their hands, forlorn passengers from a wrecked ship, clutching a few haphazardly salvaged possessions and staring in dismay at the choppy sea to which they must commit themselves.'

My best writing season starts in September. It is something to do with the new season of work, the real new year when school began or began again, and later, when you return to your office having reaffirmed your vows to be a better employee this time. The ideas come fresh, the sparkle of the days and their drawing in seems to put a fire under them, and the approach of the dark says 'Haste!' When I am not bound by teaching or lecturing it is the perfect time to travel, which is one half of writing for me. Airfares tumble, hotels have vacancies, beaches unclutter and lovers steal weekends and take city breaks. If I am work-bound I feed my travel hunger through the windows and with walking: suddenly the country is a mosaic of micro-climates. It is a happy time in the hills of Wales, my true home. Between the flies dying off and the cold closing in, farmers can ease up. If any are going to take a break they will do it between now and November. I love the days with sharp brightness in their breaking, suggestive scents and skies of many blues: pale azure and cool cerulean. E. M. Forster has a lovely description of such a day in *A Room With a View*: 'It was a Saturday afternoon, gay and brilliant after abundant rains, and the spirit of youth dwelt in it, though the season now was autumn. All that was gracious triumphed.'

I may never match that, but at my desk the words come with the quickened rhythm of the world in its turning. The literary calendar puts a spring in things with the reviews of friends' latest volumes and the new reading crop imparting urgency and inspiration. Or perhaps it is just that the muse is more bird than goddess. She shakes herself and takes wing now, as the hills change tones and no day is a settled thing. In September they are kaleidoscopes of lights and moods. I had an email from the author Niall Griffiths one day towards the end of summer, saying he had detected the coming of autumn in the wind in Wales: 'Ah how I have missed it!' he wrote.

Horatio Clare, 2016

When does autumn begin? The astronomers, followed by the almanack-makers, begin it in the third week of September, when the day and night become equal in length, and continue it until a few days short of Christmas. Many people are guided entirely by the weather of the year, and find usually that what they had thought to be early autumn is followed by another spell of summer. The rambling naturalist knows that you cannot fix dates to our seasons before they come: that they merge one into another gradually, and that a few miles north or south or the two sides of a range of hills may show a marked difference.

Some of our bird visitors left us before we began to think of autumn; but when the last of the swifts have gone, the lapwings flock and the starlings move to some other district, we know the season is about to change, and we watch for signs like the thinning of the limes, the yellowing of the elms and the browning of the beeches. As a rule, these changes are gradual; and there is still much of summer shown by the flowers and insects when the wild fruits are getting their tints of ripeness and the early fungi are beginning to appear. So, we know that our ramble in any direction will be full of interest.

Today, let us take the common, whose varied surface, broken into knolls and hollows, with thickets and copses and a few rills, should afford us a number of things that are likely to interest us. As we look away to the birchwood in the distance, the ground colour is mainly purple from the broad sheets of heather and purple heath that cover the layers of gravel. The lines of gold that come between are due to the flowers of furze – but not the common furze, whose great, thick bushes bear very few blossoms just now. The present display is chiefly that of a distant plant, the dwarf furze, not half the size of the other: and instead of making a fine show in early spring, it withholds its smaller flowers until midsummer is passed, but then keeps going until near the end of the year. It is not half the height of common furze, and many of its long, spreading branches keep close to the ground, so that we have to be wary in walking if we would avoid having our ankles stabbed by the firm, sharp spines. Often, the dwarf furze seems to show fondness for the company of heather, as it does here.

The blackthorn bushes are becoming noticeable again, for many of them are covered with fruit and promise a heavy crop of sloes later on. Their black skins are coated with the waxy 'bloom', which gives them a dull, bluish tint, and protects them from fungus attacks. Country folk will tell you that the fruit is not fit to gather until the frost has been on them; and for this reason they know them as winter-picks. Here is one of the bushes almost leafless, but not from the natural fall. We were along here a few weeks ago, when this bush was covered with hundreds of the striking caterpillars of the figure-of-eight moth, of which only a few remain: the others have crawled to the ground and become chrysalids. Judging the few that are left, you can imagine what a sight the bush made when there were hundreds of the caterpillars spreading, in full view, over it; yet, nobody else seemed to notice it. As you see, the caterpillar is quite showy, each ring having on the back a blue-grey patch with a yellow centre and four small black spots. Among the remains of dead leaves and twigs, on the ground below, there is a number of oval cocoons, in which the pale brown chrysalids are waiting for their emergence as brownish moths about October. The name is made plain on looking at the forewings, where there is a more or less clear 8 marked in white.

These bright yellow composite flowers, which are dotted freely all over this dry part of the common, are those of the long-rooted cat's-ear, one of the commonest of our weeds; but how it got its name is hard to say. It is one of that group of composites that, like the larger dandelion and the hawkweeds, have all the florets strap-shaped and with nothing to make the species distinct at a glance. We have to consider several details before deciding what is the plant's name. In this case, we note that the leaves all spring from the top of the long tapering rootstock, forming a rosette. These leaves, of which there are many, are long and narrow, with the edges scalloped or cut into pointed lobes with the tips pointing towards the root: they are bristly above and below. From the centre of the rosette rises the straight flowering stem to a height of a foot or more, branching at the upper half, each branch ending in a bright yellow flower-head an inch and a half wide. There are no leaves from the stem, only a few small bracts. Some of the earlier heads are now in fruit, crowned with a tuft of fine pale brown feathers which will carry away the beaked red-brown fruits.

Edward Step, Nature Rambles: An Introduction to Country-lore, *1930*

7

Hurrahing in Harvest

Summer ends now; now, barbarous in beauty, the stooks arise
  Around; up above, what wind-walks! what lovely behaviour
  Of silk-sack clouds! has wilder, wilful-wavier
Meal-drift moulded ever and melted across skies?

I walk, I lift up, I lift up heart, eyes,
  Down all that glory in the heavens to glean our Saviour;
  And, eyes, heart, what looks, what lips yet gave you a
Rapturous love's greeting of realer, of rounder replies?

And the azurous hung hills are his world-wielding shoulder
  Majestic – as a stallion stalwart, very-violet-sweet! –
These things, these things were here and but the beholder
  Wanting; which two when they once meet,
The heart rears wings bold and bolder
  And hurls for him, O half hurls earth for him off under his feet.

Gerard Manley Hopkins, 1877

8

Within minutes of starting work on the field side of our garden I'm joined by No. 26. She lays her broad, steamy wet nose on the top of the wall separating field from garden, and breathes encouragingly at me.

No. 26 is a Friesian heifer. Unlike the competitors in the Miss World contest, these candidates wear their numbers as ear tags, and No. 26 is hoping that I shall come up with a titbit, or hold down another elder branch for her. If I do, a thunder of hooves brings No. 22, similarly hopeful, or even No. 18, who is rather timid.

I like cows, especially Friesians. They are such shameless minders of other people's business, and gather inquisitively at anything that's going on. Initially, they press uneasily around the fringes of the large field behind our cottage, giving the impression that they would prefer to be somewhere else. Their eyes roll, and they bellow in voices of studied tragedy, perhaps at the state of the grass, which is rank.

Looking out across the brown grass of the top field – grass which to my ignorant eye must be almost uneatable for the herd which grazes it – I ponder the quantity of nourishment there can be left in it, what's left being bitten to the quick. A farmer's wife tells me that the shortage of moisture in it increases the food elements the animals are getting. I hope so. Otherwise it all looks like a long day's work for very little reward.

And I wonder again why these animals tend to bunch together as they eat. For them in their shadeless field the heat must be intense, and be increased by each other's proximity. Yet here they come, towards this house, heads down, ears and tails constantly waving, steadily chewing away. One or two have stepped aside a few paces, but the rest have stayed close, head to tail, jaws keeping up their continuous champ champ champ.

They like to spend a lot of their time bunched together in the narrow end of the lower field, between our cottage, the wall and the boundary ditch. And much as we enjoy having these creatures as neighbours, their preference for this narrow piece of the field presents certain problems. They have already spent so much time standing around on this small area that the grass there has almost given up the struggle, and much of the ground, thanks to cattle and weather, is a sea of squelch. And our bedroom window opens directly over this midden, together with its flies and farmy fragrances, especially on humid summer evenings.

I always appreciate the presence in their fields of our neighbour cows, and see them go with regretful acceptance of the fact that summer is over. But this year they have gone earlier than usual, hustled away to another field without a goodbye. The reason? They have started to break out of their home territory. A few days earlier, John had noticed that two of them were standing in the little ditch that separates the two fields and were trapped between the two fences. He rang the farmer who arrived to collect them, and to reinforce the fence on his side of the ditch at the same time. But this morning when John drew back our curtains there was a cow in the lane, wandering from verge to verge placidly going on with her life as if scaling a wall and climbing over a ditch was part of her normal routine.

This time the outcome was different. Farmer and his assistants arrived. The verdict? 'Once they've lost respect for a fence it won't keep them in. If they don't want to stay in a field you won't make them.' While John shepherded away any oncoming cars, the farming quartet steered their rebellious property out into the lane and, eventually, off to what the poet called 'pastures new' – though by this stage of the year, that's not a description that accurately describes any fields locally.

We shall miss them, noisy or quiet, when they've gone. It's always a sad moment when the last animal leaves the fields. By the end of the season the fields look tired, exhausted, spent – and, once empty, lonely, as if they miss their late occupants. For me, the dreariness of winter has finally ended once our neighbour Friesians have arrived, and their departure says 'summer is over' more convincingly than does the changing of the clocks.

Elizabeth Gardiner, 1996

August–September

Aug. 28.   Men make wheat-ricks. Mr Hale's rick fell. Vivid rain-bow.

Aug. 29.   Mr Clement begins to pick hops at Alton. *Clavaria* [club fungi] appear on the hanger.

Aug. 31.   Many moor-hens on Comb-wood pond.

Sept. 1.   Grass grows on the walks very fast. Garden beans at an end. [. . .]

Sept. 4.   Hop-picking becomes general; & the women leave their gleaning in the wheat-stubbles. Wheat grows as it stands in the shocks.

Sept. 6.   [. . .]The flying ants of the small black sort are in great agitation on the zigzag, & are leaving their nests. This business used to be carryed on in August in a warm summer. While these emigrations take place, the Hirundines fare deliciously on the female ants full of eggs. Hop-picking becomes general; & all the kilns, or as they are called in some counties, *oasts*, are in use. Hops dry brown, & are pretty much subject this year to vinny, or mould.

Sept. 8.   Sowed thirteen rods, on the twelfth part of an acre of grass ground in my own upper Ewel close with 50 pounds weight of Gypsum; also thirteen rods in Do with 50 pounds weight of lime: thirteen rods more in Do with 50 pounds weight of wood & peat-ashes:

and four rods more on D^o with peat-dust. All these sorts of manures were sown by Bro^r T. W. on very indifferent grass in the way of experiment.

Sept. 9. As most of the second brood of Hirundines are now out, the young on fine days congregate in considerable numbers on the church & tower: & it is remarkable that tho' the generality sit on the battlements & roof, yet many *bang* or cling for some time by their claws against the surface of the walls in a manner not practised at any other time of their remaining with us. By far the greater number of these amusing birds are house-martins, not swallows, which congregate more on trees. A writer in the Gent. Mag. supposes that the chilly mornings & evenings, at this decline of the year, begin to influence the feelings of the young broods; & that they cluster thus in the hot sunshine to prevent their blood from being benumbed, & themselves from being reduced to a state of untimely torpidity.

Sept. 11. On this day my niece Anne Woods was married to Mr John Hounsom, who encreases my nephews, & nieces to the number of 59. Mr John White came from Salisbury.

Sept. 12. Began to light fires in the parlour. J. W. left us.

Sept. 13. The stream at Gracious street, which fails every dry summer, has run briskly all this year; & seems now to be equal to the current from Wellhead. The rocky channel up the hollow-lane towards Rood has also run with water for months: nor has my great water-tub been dry the summer through.

Sept. 14.   From London three gallons of French brandy, & two gallons of Jamaica rum.

Sept. 15.   Hop women complain of the cold.

Reverend Gilbert White, The Naturalist's Journal, *1792*

Towards the end of August our Highland landscape is swathed in a royal blanket. The heather blooms quickly; whole hillsides are repainted in many shades of purple, sometimes almost in the blink of an eye. It is a febrile transformation which stretches into early September. Countless millions of tiny flowers and little bells open and their heavy scent fills the late summer air, when the atmosphere becomes intoxicating and somnolent. Hints of autumn flicker in and out. On some days the light is golden, and pours across the hills like honey; on others, it is sharp, bright and crisply cold. The nights are no longer white and pearl grey, but darken swiftly.

In the croft fields wild flowers are setting seeds. Insects dart about in search of remaining nectar, their wings white, yellow and orange, some spotted or banded, others translucent, fragile and opalescent. Birds, pale breasted but with colourful caps and bright feathers, chatter and sing as they skim along the river banks and through the fields from seed head to seed head. On the few overhead wires, swallows gather. Their nests in the byre have been tidied and in between the chattering pauses they fly, dipping and flashing across the river, swerving over the fields. On these end-of-summer, sometimes warm days, the air shimmers; insects cascade and billow as myriad birds rush to feed.

The land luxuriates in those snatched days of golden and rose-pink warmth and especially in the scented gift of calm evenings which come in colours of hazy blue, crimson, coral, copper and rose. When the sun finally sets there is a sudden firing of turquoise light which glows like an unexpected glaze on pottery taken freshly from the kiln, so that for a few moments it outshines all else, until it too dissipates. But it is a cold light. It warns of change. Autumn is coming.

The heather's bloom does not last long, two, perhaps three weeks if the weather is kind. But then the flowers turn to dusty gold. Greens and purples give way to bronze and umber. Soon the fields turn egg-custard yellow with sprinklings of cinnamon where terracotta seed heads of sorrel, burnt-umber plantains and ground-ginger rushes still stand proud. In late afternoon sun the machair now looks more Mediterranean, the dying dryness of flower petals and seed heads weaving into the copper and rust of bracken fronds and the waving grasses.

On the mountains, tussocks of deer grass open out like the coat of a red deer hind parted to reveal the speckled paleness of her under-fur. Almost hidden in the heather, red leaves of tormentil trail like bracelets made of rubies. Sphagnum mosses glow in absinthe and claret, tiny plum-coloured berries of bog rosemary resting on the top of their spongy cushions. Along the shore, close to the croft, russet and orange colour the boulders while on the sands strings of mermaid's tresses mingle with the auburn feathers of dabberlocks and sugar kelp. Above the strand-line, sorrel seed heads stand like tall, iron-rust swords or flames of vermillion.

Then suddenly the swallows have gone. The air is quieter for their departure, but other, more measured voices fill the spaces: robins singing quiet laments of farewell and longing, separation and loss. Even though I know they are really songs of fighting, boundaries and ownership, and I admire their feistiness, to me they are heralds of summer's flight to the south. Much higher, in the open spaces above the fields, there are new sounds. Geese begin to arrive, windborne squadrons of raiders from the north, honking and gliding in wedges, and then landing in guffawing gaggles in the meadows by the river. Their calls are powerful, evoking further pangs of melancholy, but they do not stay long. Our croft is one service station on their aerial motorway to their food-filled estuarine winter holiday homes. They feed vigorously and rest. Then, at some unseen signal, they lift and rise up over the hills to slowly disappear from view.

In the woodlands the first trees to betray summer are silver birches: splashes of yellow dapple their fine, shimmering greenery. Here and there, long wavering larch tresses begin to change from deep green to orange and ochre. Gradually the azurite, ultramarine and verdigris of late summer is overlain by Byzantine bronze, copper and gold, and even on days of dull, grey cloud, the oranges and deep russet reds glow as if hot. Slowly, steadily leaves begin to fall: silver birch and aspen leaves descend in gentle cascades like confetti, oak, sycamore and beech leaves spin down crunchily. Hedges are stippled with blackberry and rosehip, woodlands with berry and nut. Fungi of varying size, shape and shade surprise us with their sudden appearance, sprouting here, opening there, tucked alongside old fence posts, logs and branches. And each day, as a little more light is lost, trees, shrubs, herbs and grasses defiantly erupt in volcanic colours to compensate for the coming of the dark and cold.

As September progresses, autumn fiercely rushes towards us in the chaos of Atlantic storms. They are heralded at first by high, thin, white ripples of pearlescent clouds with rainbowed iridescent edges. Soon strong westerly winds blow hard and wet, returning again and again and again to strip trees, churning leaves into skirmishing maelstroms of colour. Summer lochs and coastal seas of turquoise and quicksilver are transformed into pulsating gunmetal grey, cobalt and aquamarine, topped by high jumping horses of brilliantine and white. The shore becomes furious then; sand, shells, stones and ocean detritus are hurled about to crash down into high mounds and ridges. Across the machair mists and mellow fruitfulness are torn apart; birds take to the air and are thrown about like charcoal-black scraps of paper burnt on a fire and caught in updraughts. When the rains come to accompany the winds our rivers and burns convulse and carry leaves, twigs and branches down to the sea. The coastal Highlands become a battleground between land, air and water.

But then, above the tumult in the sea and skies, other, wilder voices of war are heard: stags are corralling their harems and defiantly readying themselves for battle. Their roars and bellows ricochet from crag and hill and echo along the riverbanks. It is the rut. Wild, glorious autumn is here.

Annie Worsley, 2016

Autumn Again

These last days I have spent
doing nothing but reading
your John Clare and the name itself
has come to change meaning.

It is still up on Coombe Hill
and there is late summer sun
boiling the reservoir I'm fishing
today, trying to re-belong.

I regret the fidget in my heart,
my firm-set bad timing,
the inaccuracy of my cast.
The forty-odd miles north of this swim.

Will Burns, 2016

Autumn has been coming on for a while. Even in mid August the signs were all there: colder nights and early morning dew; blackberries deepening and swelling; the sycamore seeds poised for launch. Soon it was the turn of the rosebay willowherb that had bolted through the summer like a lanky teenager. Its perfection past, now it was going to seed, along with the creeping and spear thistles; the architectural spires and precision points gave way to softness as they all shed that downy fluff that you just have to pull off and hold. In our back garden the resident blackbird, distinguishable by his white tail feathers, has made himself scarce. I tell my youngest daughter that Morris (as he's been named) has gone off to fatten up in the woods, and have a little holiday just like we do. 'He doesn't need to do that, Mummy. We've got enough plums and apples falling here. *And* the elderberries.' (Jemima is a natural forager and has developed a taste for elderberries – in fact, for anything she can find to eat outside. She picked at the elderflowers and ate them, then watched the green berries daily, willing them to turn purple and capsize.)

'When's he coming back?'

'I don't know, but I'm sure he will,' I tell her. 'I hope we can recognise him though, he will have moulted. Some people say this makes them hide away.'

'Like a bad hair day?'

'Kind of, but worse. A bad feather day could affect his

20

flying. It could make him feel unsafe, more exposed. But you don't need to worry about him, he can take care of himself.'

You can't blame the garden birds for wanting a taste of the wild; for some, of course, our limited patch is only ever just a small part of their feeding ground. The woods and hedgerows are providing an abundance of fruit this year, and the attraction is obvious. By the start of September the sloes are plump and blue already, and the blackberries have been burgeoning for weeks, at times dissolving on the brambles, being too plentiful to be gathered in. Human efforts at blackberry picking seem to be half-hearted this year (my family aside). It must have something to do with how August has dripped its way into an early wet September, the autumnal damp well-established before its rightful time. The badgers in the woods are not sick of blackberries yet – their little latrine pits contain piles of purple dung, full of the tell-tale seeds.

The dog needs his walks despite the rain and so we continue to haunt the landscape. We're out in fine drizzle once again and I can't help thinking how quiet the place is now. I share the village with more than two thousand other people, and the woods with just a few; these days I can go for a whole walk without seeing a soul. I think most people are lying when they say they walk their dog at least once a day. But it's the birdsong I'm missing. It's understood that birds sing less in the rain, and then of course their seasonal need to sing has past – having found a territory and had their young, their year is complete. H. G. Alexander suggests that blackbirds will sing more in the rain, but presumably not when they've stopped the choral ritual anyway. That aside, I know there is a beauty in quietness and I need to retrain my ear.

I have noticed another change inside these woods – the trees seem to be turning faster here than on the outside. I appreciate the gloom could make the leaves show up more when they come to rest on the dark floor, and yet I think there is a little more to it. This is no vast wood – in places it's little more than a modest strip of broadleaf woodland between fields, just twenty metres across. Daylight can filter in through the canopy overhead and dapple the floor with sunshine. It creeps in from the outer edges, too. But perhaps the trees here register the arrival of autumn before the rest, for some are contained within the canopy and have far less exposure to sunlight.

There is a distinct smell in the air now that I haven't smelt for almost a year. It's hard to locate exactly – I don't know if it's the damp rotting wood, the overripe fruit, or the moss that's growing more brightly and more densely as it soaks up the rain. I suspect it's a combination, and will intensify with the fungi that grow around here and the soon-to-be rotting leaves. When autumn is over there will be a new harvest of sorts, as the wild flowers begin working their way up through this newly replenished soil; old leaf-fall provides the nourishment now, but in time this year's nutrients will be recycled into leaf and flower.

I head home feeling that the woodland harvest is just beginning, with our own ingathering a little ahead of nature's own yield. In the Celtic calendar August marked the start of autumn, with three months of 'Harvest'. Perhaps this is a more accurate way to look at it, for our own harvest-time is just a small part of the story, and bound up in a delicate balance extending far beyond the edges of the field.

Caroline Greville, 2016

Fungi. In the damp weather of autumn the fungus tribe become very numerous, and often are the first phenomena which remind us of the decline of summer and the approach of cooler season, when

Libra dies somni pares ubi fecerit horas.

There is something remarkable about the growth of fungi. Some fungi appear here and there springing up in places where they are least expected, and where they have perhaps never grown before. How do the seeds come in such places? A learned cryptogamist once said, he thought their semina floated in the air, and were carried up into the clouds, and wafted along with them, and deposited by fogs on the earth's surface. Is there any particular aspect or side of trees more obnoxious to the growth of parasitical fungi than others?

Thomas Furly Forster, The Pocket Encyclopaedia of Natural Phenomena, *published 1827*

As the blaze of summer flowers slowly fades, deep in the Chilterns the twinkling purple stars of Chiltern gentians start to appear on the chalk grassland.

Like the orchids in summer, Chiltern gentians seem too elegant and exquisite to be growing wild in our countryside. Clusters of purple star-shaped flowers stand proud above the short grass, each with five pointed petals around a delicate centre of fine white hairs. The county flower of Buckinghamshire, it's listed as nationally scarce and vulnerable, being found, as the name suggests, only in certain parts of the Chilterns. One such place is Yoesden, a nature reserve acquired by the Berkshire, Buckinghamshire and Oxfordshire Wildlife Trust after a major appeal in 2014. The site is considered one of the most important areas of chalk grassland in the Chilterns. With up to forty plant species in a single square metre, chalk grassland has often been likened to Europe's answer to the tropical rainforest. This wildlife-rich habitat is in serious decline though, with much of it lost to farming. Saved from the plough by its steep sloping bank, Yoesden is now a reserve full of surprises all year round.

We follow the path through the trees, stepping through an archway of blackthorn onto the top corner of the bank. Even the children pause for a moment, stopped in their tracks by the spectacular view. We are spectators on the top step of an overgrown amphitheatre, waiting for the performance to begin. Ancient woodland stands guard along the top of the slope and the hills seem to roll all around us. A sleepy village nestles amongst the trees in the valley below, only visible by its chimney pots and twelfth-century church tower. Red kites soar through the sky, ever watchful, while green woodpeckers call their laughing yaffle from the nearby woods.

As if nature is working her way through the rainbow, the pale yellow primroses in spring have been replaced by the pink common spotted orchids and delicate blue harebells of summer. But by the beginning of September the colour purple is most definitely the star of the show, with the majestic Chiltern gentians sparkling along the warm chalk slope. As we wander through this amazing herb garden it soon becomes clear that we're far from alone and the site is alive with all manner of insects. The smoky wings of chalkhill blue butterflies drift past and a speckled wood sunbathes ahead of us in the middle of the path, taking flight as we approach, just to settle in the same spot once we're gone. A hornet buzzes past, making us stand to attention and keep a respectful distance. The children are fascinated by the sight of a tiny crab spider lurking in a flower head, ready to pounce on any unsuspecting prey. They're amazed that she can change colour to blend into her surroundings; a chameleon in our midst. Crickets and grasshoppers chirp and whirr all around us, each species producing its individual song. The children are looking and listening for one in particular though, the great green bush-cricket, a prehistoric-looking creature with huge, exaggerated features and a song like a sewing machine. It's a highlight of any visit, especially if they can find one obliging enough to sit on a hand for a moment before taking flight. I catch sight of a flash of electric blue out of the corner of my eye and I'm lucky enough to see one of our most stunning, but also most rare butterflies, the Adonis blue.

Before we realise it, we've meandered our way across to the far side of the bank, but there is still one more treat before we leave. Heading into the woods, we follow a path until the trees open out to reveal a hidden glade known as the 'hole in the woods'. The pincushion blooms of devil's-bit scabious sway in the breeze on their slender stems, covering the glade in a rippling, purple sea. The flowers are clearly a much loved source of nectar and each one seems to play host to a bee or butterfly. The children are enchanted by the legend that the devil was so angry about the medicinal properties of this plant that he tried to get rid of it by biting off the roots, leaving the plant with short, stubby roots and the name devil's-bit scabious. It's a wonderful finale to our walk around this remarkable place.

Sue Croxford, 2016

Flies, and various sorts of volatile insects, become more troublesome, and sting and bite more than usual before, as well as in the intervals of rainy weather, particularly in autumn, when they are very numerous, and often become great nuisance. This observation applies to several sorts of flies. The horseflies likewise of all sorts are more troublesome before the fall of rain, and particularly when the weather is warm.

Thomas Furly Forster, The Pocket Encyclopaedia
of Natural Phenomena, *published 1827*

It was macabre from a distance; a pure white, human-sized skull glowing out from the darkness of the woodland glade. My son whooped with delight and charged up to the perfect sphere, raising it above his head like a trophy. Out in the sunlight, we inhaled its sweet fungus scent. It was a giant puffball mushroom, the size of a football. It was no longer sinister; it was less like a murder victim's skull and more like a snowman's head, cool and heavy in our hands.

Since having children, I have lost my mushroom foraging confidence. Poisoning myself would be rather inconvenient (especially for those around me), but to make the children ill or worse through mistaken mushroom identity would be devastating and unforgivable.

The giant puffball is my safe foraging mushroom because for me it is so easily and reliably recognisable. With a young specimen, bigger than a grapefruit and perfectly white throughout, I can be utterly sure of what it is. They can grow even larger than your head, although the orb becomes lumpen and yellowed, like a whale's brain imagined. To find out if it is OK to eat, you need to slice it in half. If the flesh inside has lost its solid white, fresh-driven-snow-like appearance and turned beige or yellow, then it won't taste good. Luckily, it will still be ideal for a messy game of fungi football.

I've never managed to find a puffball on purpose. The best plan is to go blackberry picking and keep your eyes open for strange white objects in grassland or deciduous woodland edges.

However, they do often regrow at the same spot each year, so if you get lucky one year, it pays to return the following autumn. Indeed, it is something of a miracle that we aren't surrounded by puffballs, because inside a large, mature puffball, when it has turned brown and dry, there can be more than a trillion spores.

We returned home with our heavy bounty. It was big enough to provide several meals. First, simply fried with garlic and butter and served on toast, the texture somewhere between firm tofu and a savoury marshmallow. The next day it was cut into discs for puffball pizza. Each disc was sprinkled with olive oil and grilled on each side until soft, then topped with tomato sauce and cheese and returned to the grill until golden and bubbly. Pudding was blackberry muffins, still warm from the oven.

Our foraged food, found and shared as a family, roots us into our environment more deeply than ever.

Kate Blincoe, 2016

Threshing Morning

On an apple-ripe September morning
Through the mist-chill fields I went
With a pitchfork on my shoulder
Less for use than for devilment.

The threshing mill was set-up, I knew,
In Cassidy's haggard last night,
And we owed them a day at the threshing
Since last year. O it was delight

To be paying bills of laughter
And chaffy gossip in kind
With work thrown in to ballast
The fantasy-soaring mind.

As I crossed the wooden bridge I wondered
As I looked into the drain
If ever a summer morning should find me
Shovelling up eels again.

And I thought of the wasps' nest in the bank
And how I got chased one day
Leaving the drag and the scraw-knife behind,
How I covered my face with hay.

AUTUMN

The wet leaves of the cocksfoot
Polished my boots as I
Went round by the glistening bog-holes
Lost in unthinking joy.

I'll be carrying bags today, I mused,
The best job at the mill
With plenty of time to talk of our loves
As we wait for the bags to fill . . .

Maybe Mary might call round . . .
And then I came to the haggard gate,
And I knew as I entered that I had come
Through fields that were part of no earthly estate.

Patrick Kavanagh, 1943

Swallows are gathering on the telegraph wires, and it's clear that summer is coming to an end. Everywhere, our native wildlife is preparing to hunker down for the colder months ahead – and hedgerows play a crucial role for many creatures. Hazel dormice breed late in the summer specifically to take advantage of the natural bounty, their tiny young tucked up in nests of beautifully woven strips of honeysuckle bark. Wood mice stock their leaf-lined larders with nuts and elderberries, and I've watched badgers snuffling under crab apple trees in search of windfalls. Comma and Red Admiral butterflies bask in the last warmth of the summer sun and join lazy wasps in getting drunk on fermenting fruit juices as the berries begin to decay. In the field margins, goldfinches balance delicately on slender-stemmed groundsel, spiky thistles and tall, prickly teasels, winkling out the seeds with their sensitive beaks.

October is usually well underway when the whole hedgerow begins to change into winter hues. The glossy red and purple fruits and berries are not the only splash of colour in the hedge at this time of year. Bramble leaves are often the first to show a tinge of scarlet despite many often still flowering, with promise of more fruit in the coming weeks. By comparison, some trees and bushes seem to fade to brown without displaying any fiery tints, but the field maples rarely disappoint and ash trees laden with keys, which rustle in the breeze, turn a wonderful shade of yellow. It won't be long until the leaves are gone altogether, and the bare branches await their new green foliage in spring.

As November beckons, the days turn colder and the first frosts glitter in the ever paler morning sunlight, highlighting every strand of spider's silk hung from the brittle stalks of hogweed. Sloes are reaching their prime, the icy mornings sweetening them. There are fewer insects around now. Ladybirds, lacewings and peacock butterflies have sought out the shelter of our homes and garden sheds to wait out the winter, but a few lingering hornets are making the most of any remaining fruit they can find. It's on days like this that the first winter migrants arrive, and we hear the unmistakeable cackling call of fieldfares and the peep of migrating redwings at night. Together with our native blackbirds and thrushes they flock to the laden hawthorn bushes, methodically stripping them of berries.

As the seasons progress, the needs of different species change. In autumn, the shrubs and trees making up the hedgerow have matured and their fruits bear seeds of future generations. For them, autumn is a season of productivity. But for the species that feed on them, autumn is a season of necessity. They need to eat plentifully while the food is available, to put on weight before the cold of winter takes hold. Without the vital resources that the hedgerow provides, many species would struggle as the days grow shorter and our British countryside would be an altogether less colourful place.

Alice Hunter, 2016

September

Sept. 16.   Dᴿ Chandler's Bantam sow brought him this last summer a large litter of pigs, several of which were not cloven-footed, but had their toes joined to-gether. For tho' on the upper part of the foot there was somewhat of a suture, or division; yet below in the soles the toes were perfectly united; & on some of the hind legs there was a solid hoof like that of a colt. The feet of the sow are completely cloven. Mᴿ Ray in his *Synopsis animalium quadrupedum* takes no notice of this singular variety; but *Linnaeus* in his *Systema Naturae* says, 'Varietas frequens Upsaliae Suis domestici simper *monunguli*: in ceteris eadem species.'

Sept. 17.   Gathered-in the white pippins, about a bushel: many were blown down last week. Oats housed.

Sept. 19.   Rain. Hops become very brown, & damaged. The hop-pickers are wet through every day.

Sept. 21.   On this day Monarchy was abolished at Paris by the National Convention; & France became a Republic!

Sept. 22.   As I have questioned men that frequent coppices respecting Fern-owls, which they have not seen or heard of late; there is reason to suspect that they have withdrawn themselves, as well as the fly-catchers, & black-caps, about the beginning of this month.

Where timber lies felled among the bushes, & covert, wood-men tell me, that fern-owls love to sit upon the logs of an evening: but what their motive is does not appear.

Sept. 23. My Bantam chickens, which have been kept in the scullery every night till now for fear of the rats, that carried away the first brood from the brew-house, went up last week to the beam over the stable. The earnest & early propensity of the *Gallinae* to roost on high is very observable; & discovers a strong dread impressed on their spirits respecting vermin that may annoy them on the ground during the hours of darkness. Hence poultry, if left to themselves & not housed, will perch, the winter through on yew-trees & fir-trees; & turkies & Guinea-fowls, heavy as they are, get up into apple trees; pheasants also in woods sleep on trees to avoid foxes:– while pea-fowls climb to the tops of the highest trees round their owner's house for security, let the weather be ever so cold or blowing. Partridges, it is true, roost on the ground, not having the faculty of perching; but then the same fear prevails in their minds; for through apprehensions from pole-cats, weasels, & stoats, they never trust themselves to coverts; but nestle together in the midst of large fields, far removed from hedges & coppices, which they love to haunt/frequent in the day; & where at that season they can skulk more secure from the ravages of rapacious birds. As to ducks, & geese, their aukward splay web-feet forbid them to settle on trees: they therefore, in the hours of darkness & danger, betake themselves to their own element the water, where amidst large lakes & pools, like ships riding at anchor, they float the whole night long in peace, & security.

Sept. 25.   Men begin to bag hops. Celeri comes in. Vine-leaves turn purple.

Sept. 30.   There is a remarkable hill on the downs near *Lewes* in *Sussex*, known by the name of *Mount Carburn* [Caburn], which over-looks that town, & affords a most engaging prospect of all the country round, besides several views of the sea. On the very summit of this exalted promontory, & amidst the trenches of its Danish [British] camp, there haunts a species of wild Bee, making its nest in the chalky soil. When people approach the place, these insects begin to be alarmed, & with a sharp & hostile sound dash, & strike round the heads & faces of intruders. I have often been interrupted myself while contemplating the grandeur of the scenery around me, & have thought myself in danger of being stung:– and have heard my Brother *Benjamin* say, that he & his daughter *Rebecca* were driven from the spot by the fierce menaces of these angry insects.

Reverend Gilbert White, The Naturalist's Journal, *1792*

Dusk, when the edges of all things blur. A time of mauve and moonlight, of shapeshiftings and stirrings, of magic. It's my favourite time of day.

Nocturnal wildlife has a special fascination; it usually lives out of sight beneath the radar of our everyday, human lives. We pull on our fleeces, let the camp-fire die down and steal into the woods. I hear the moan of the pump house and the faint laughter of children in the camping field. We make our way quietly down the woodland path, old beechmast crunching underfoot, midges fussing about our faces. The moon rises up in the east, spilling light over a few steely clouds. The sky deepens to a twilight blue. It is balmy and a gentle breeze lifts the black lacy hands of the canopy in a silent dance. Below us the woodland floor falls away in a confusion of ferns, red campion, bramble and ivy. Somewhere down below is the badger sett we discovered earlier in the day, inconspicuous unless you are close by. The smooth hummocks, discarded bedding and well-worn paths meandering off through the trees are tell-tale signs. It's intriguing to think that a badger family might be slumbering beneath our feet.

We wait. The ground is damp; it has rained in the last few days and the badgers will be out foraging for earthworms. They emerge earlier in the evenings in autumn for food and bedding. We listen. I crouch in the spiky twigs of a hawthorn bush in a pocket of darkness, fingers in the earth to steady myself. The close smell of earth and leaf litter. My partner stands motionless a few metres away, back against a beech. We wait and listen, wait and listen. Anticipation. Darkness creeps into all spaces, rich animal darkness wraps around us.

Japanese folklore has it that badgers can shapeshift into humans and sing songs. Or they may change themselves into trees, stones, comets, drum on their bellies as pranksters, lure unsuspecting observers into ditches and swamps. This evening we have been lured into the woods at dusk by our own curiosity.

The shadows rustle. The sound becomes a movement in the corner of my eye. Do my ears and eyes deceive me? There is a movement to my left along the path I am sure. I dare to turn my head but fear my clothes will rustle. I can just make out my partner, who has turned towards me. He is mouthing something; he too has sensed a movement, a badger close by.

A little piece of grey-garbed night is trundling towards us, quite unaware of our presence. It is a little unsettling to think he could run into me on this path. He – I call it *he* for convenience – snuffles the earth, hesitates but seems unbothered; badgers rule these woods. And he is so, so quiet. Now I can see the white stripes on his face, his open gaze, as curious as I am. There is something humorous, almost comical about him. He bows and lifts his head, sniffing the air; badgers have reasonable night vision but a great sense of smell. He seems unfazed and comes closer. So close is he now that I could reach out and touch him from my place in the shadows.

I stay as still as I can in the hawthorn. It is thrilling to be so close to a wild animal, to be in *their* space.

The badger is just one foot away now and I am tense and trying not to shake. The moment is long; I know I will need to move soon. I make a slight noise and give myself away. The badger stands stock still for a second and then, with a blur of grey, he hurries off into the night. I sigh, but I'm smiling. Smiling to myself in the darkness.

Alexi Francis, 2016

*O*n the Harvest Moon and the Hunter's Moon. The nearest Moon to the autumnal equinox is called the Harvest Moon: it rises nearer to the same each succeeding night at this time of year than it does at any other: it has received its cognomen in autumn only, on account probably of its use to the farmers, when pressed for time with the ingathering of the harvest. The cause of this phenomenon is the Moon's being in the signs ♓ and ♈ at the time of the full, in which she is during this and the succeeding month. The October Moon is called the Hunter's Moon. It is well known that the signs ♓ and ♈ rise making the smallest, and ♎ and ♍ rise making the greatest angle with the horizon; and *vice versa* with respect to setting. Now the Moon, whose orbit is nearly parallel to the ecliptic, is the full in ♓ and ♈ in September and October, consequently, rising in those months, she makes the least angle with the horizon, and therefore rises nearer to the same time every evening.

Thomas Furly Forster, The Pocket Encyclopaedia of Natural Phenomena, *published 1827*

For an ecologist, fieldwork is a pleasure. In autumn it is a bitter-sweet pleasure. The day itself will be a quiet joy like other field days, but the weakening sun, lengthening shadows and changing colours remind us that such pleasures will soon be curtailed, until spring, when buds will start bursting forth once more.

It was in search of such bittersweet pleasure that, some years ago, I set out with a colleague, Victoria, on a research trip to survey some lime trees. We were studying two British species of limes that grow in close proximity in the same wood, trying to understand how separate they were. Did they co-exist as two distinct species, small-leaved lime and large-leaved lime? Or did they take advantage of this proximity, of overlapping flowering times and shared pollinators, to cross-fertilise and merge into one?

A line of isolated magical woods, roughly situated on the English–Welsh border from Shropshire down to the lower reaches of the Wye Valley, is where this question is best answered and hence our destination. On this day we were in Worcestershire. Bordered by hills to the east and west, split by two of the great English rivers, the Severn and the Avon, and retaining a mixture of grassland, arable fields, orchards and woodland, it is perhaps the quintessential English lowland county. Its patchwork would still be recognised by Piers Plowman as the one he viewed from the Malverns in the fourteenth century. Travelling through the narrow lanes, autumn had clearly begun to show its hand. Late morning and there was still dew on the vegetation, while in the hedgerows green was beginning to retreat from the leaves.

41

The Knapp and Papermill Nature Reserve is a microcosm of the county. It is entered via a narrow path that ascends up a short rise to reveal an old orchard, where burnished apples are starting to fall from the boughs. This gives way to grassland, untouched by the intrusion of late twentieth-century agriculture, although the season was leaving its mark. The straw-coloured grass dropped its seed as we walked through it to admire more closely the purple-red of the knapweed flowers. To the left is a narrow stream. To the right is a steep slope, bearing a wood that is a relic of the virtually continuous verdant cover that once sprawled over the land. It is this wood, or rather its limes and their sexuality, that we had come to study.

The English have a confused relationship with woodlands. Plans to limit public access or to grub out parts of them for development are seen as an outrage, evoking strong resistance. At the same time, we see them as sources of danger; from childhood we are warned of them, through fairy stories, as places where people are easily lost or abducted. Nature resides there, but a nature that is wild and sometimes life-threatening.

Individual trees also elicit a strong emotional response, and limes are among the most beloved. When I first started to study them, I thought this was a product of their rarity. They are invariably found in special, secretive places; a relic of pre-human Britain, when such trees covered most of the land. Thus to find limes is to briefly glimpse the world as it appeared to our ancestors.

This cannot be the full story, however. Lime-lovers abound even without this historical ecological perspective. Perhaps it is the trees themselves: typically immense structures with dense canopies of abundant foliage, supported by huge, stout trunks, that in turn rely upon rock-grasping roots. These trees continue to exist as they have done for centuries, roots and leaves miraculously extracting the chemicals for life; they have broken time's arrow and to encounter them is to gain a brief glimpse of immortality.

Perhaps our affection is an echo of the folklore that surrounds them. Across various parts of Europe the tree represents justice, health, fertility and romance. In Germany, the romantic association inspired the famous medieval poem *Unter der Linden* by Walter von der Vogelweide, which tells of the secret tryst between a knight and a peasant girl. Perhaps that connection lies in the shape of the leaves themselves – photosynthetic hearts suspended overhead.

It is these hearts we had come to collect, to extract DNA and thus determine the relationship between the trees. We also mapped their locations, measure trunk size and growth form to help form a fuller picture. A picture of past unions and tangled relationships. We carefully paced out our survey area. The steep rocky slope made movement through the wood difficult, but once we found our targets we fell to work quickly. Although we had never been in the field together previously, we fell into an easy rhythm. Taking each tree in turn, we swiftly, almost wordlessly took on our roles. Find the tree, number it, slip the tape around it, measure, record, take a trowel full of soil, place in bag, seal, label, match the leaves to the trunk, collect, place in bag, seal, breathe deeply and move on to the next one.

We continued to work in this way, slipping through the wood and gradually losing sense of time or, indeed, of anything beyond the trees themselves, until we had a full set of samples. Collecting done, we sat and rested under one of our trees. A couple of cast-off leaves spiralled down in front of us and the day slowly came back into focus.

Paul Ashton, 2016

To come to Chilworth, which lies on the south side of St. Martha's Hill, most people would have gone along the level road to Guildford, and come round through Shawford under the hills; but we, having seen enough of streets and turnpikes, took across over Merrow Down, where the Guildford race-course is, and then mounted the 'Surrey Hills,' so famous for the prospects they afford. Here we looked back over Middlesex, and into Buckinghamshire and Berkshire, away towards the north-west, into Essex and Kent towards the east, over part of Sussex to the south, and over part of Hampshire to the west and south-west. We are here upon a bed of chalk, where the downs always afford good sheep food. We steered for St. Martha's Chapel, and went round at the foot of the lofty hill on which it stands. This brought us down the side of a steep hill, and along a bridle-way, into the narrow and exquisitely beautiful vale of Chilworth, where we were to stop for the night. This vale is skirted partly by woodlands and partly by sides of hills tilled as corn fields. The land is excellent, particularly towards the bottom. Even the arable fields are in some places, towards their tops, nearly as steep as the roof of a tiled house; and where the ground is covered with woods the ground is still more steep. Down the middle of the vale there is a series of ponds, or small *lakes*, which meet your eye, here and there, through the trees. Here are some very fine farms, a little strip of meadows, some hop-gardens, and the lakes have given rise to the establishment of powder-mills and paper-mills. The trees of all sorts grow well here; and coppices yield poles for the hop-gardens and wood to make charcoal for the powder-mills.

They are sowing wheat here, and the land, owing to the fine summer that we have had, is in a very fine state. The rain, too, which, yesterday, fell here in great abundance, has been just in time to make a really good wheat-sowing season. The turnips all the way that we have come, are good. Rather backward in some places; but in sufficient quantity upon the ground, and there is yet a good while for them to grow. All the fall fruit is excellent, and in great abundance. The grapes are as good as those raised under glass. The apples are much richer than in ordinary years. The crop of hops has been very fine here, as well as everywhere else. The crop is not only large, but good in quality. They expect to get *six* pounds a hundred for them at Weyhill Fair. That is *one* more than I think they will get.

September 1822

William Cobbett, Rural Rides, *1830*

It is just before dawn on a misty autumnal morning and the air is slightly chilled. My local wetland, Barton Fields in Abingdon, becomes unfamiliar, ethereal, and breathtakingly beautiful. The dawn chorus ceased in July, but the melancholic sweetness of a robin's song suddenly fills the morning air, and my heart, as I continue on the grassy path.

The sky turns a soft pink as the sun begins to rise through the mist. As I pass a bramble on the opposite side of a stream, close to the Thames, a movement catches my eye. I assume it is a moorhen, as I have seen them climbing brambles above other streams. But this bird is brown and grey with a long reddish beak. A water rail! I wonder if an otter has spooked it? Otters will take these birds. I find distinctive, five-toed otter footprints in a damp muddy patch, but the owner remains elusive.

The following day it is warm and sunny as I head out mid-morning to walk through Abbey Fishponds. As I approach a bramble bush laden with ripe blackberries, I slow down and walk silently. I had noted the head of a small mammal fleeing into the depths of this bush as I returned home on the previous day. During that fleeting moment it looked like a bank vole, rather than a wood mouse with its upright ears. Now I wait silently and motionlessly for about twenty minutes. At last, much to my delight, a bank vole emerges out of the depths of the brambles into the sunlight almost in front of me. I stand, enchanted by this wild, charismatic character. Such a special, Beatrix Potter moment. What a privilege!

The bank vole deftly avoids the thorns to sit in the bramble by its chosen blackberry. It does not bite through the stem, as I have seen water voles do, and then rush off with it. A blackberry is rather a large feast for this mouse-sized mammal. It clasps the blackberry in its small hands and begins eating its clustered drupelets with relish, its dark, appealing eyes shining. Then it cleans its teeth with deft paws and eats a leaf before disappearing swiftly into the depths of the bramble once more.

Bank voles do not hibernate and are active during the day and night. They become nocturnal in the summer months, so the best chance of seeing one is in the autumn. This is because their numbers plummet in the winter to a low during April when the breeding season begins. Breeding continues until October.

Tawny owls live nearby and rely on small mammals as part of their diet for their own survival. This bramble bush was not only supplying bank voles and birds with autumnal food. It was there, one early autumn morning, that I saw a young tawny owl sitting on a branch close to the trunk of a bleached, dead tree above the reed-bed. The reeds surrounded the tree, almost reaching the branch the owl was sitting on. It was surprisingly well camouflaged among the light brown, feather-like common reed heads on their sun-dried stems. The owlet had left its nest because its parents were no longer feeding it. It sat in the tree, looking as if it was not quite certain what to do next. I left, concerned about disturbing it, and when I returned a couple of hours later to check that it was OK, was heartened to find that it had flown to find a new home.

I love this season of gradual withdrawal. It is not only a visible withdrawal by nature, but a subtle inner withdrawal, too; a slow, imperceptible retreat into ourselves. A season of rest and quietness as the days shorten. A chance to recharge the soul after a spring and summer of almost constant activity.

Jo Cartmell, 2016

Ode to the West Wind

I

O wild West Wind, thou breath of Autumn's being,
Thou from whose unseen presence the leaves dead
Are driven like ghosts from an enchanter fleeing,

Yellow, and black, and pale, and hectic red,
Pestilence-stricken multitudes! O thou
Who chariotest to their dark wintry bed

The winged seeds, where they lie cold and low,
Each like a corpse within its grave, until
Thine azure sister of the Spring shall blow

Her clarion o'er the dreaming earth, and fill
(Driving sweet buds like flocks to feed in air)
With living hues and odours plain and hill;

Wild Spirit, which art moving everywhere;
Destroyer and preserver; hear, O hear!

II

Thou on whose stream, 'mid the steep sky's commotion,
Loose clouds like earth's decaying leaves are shed,
Shook from the tangled boughs of heaven and ocean,

Angels of rain and lightning! there are spread
On the blue surface of thine airy surge,
Like the bright hair uplifted from the head

Of some fierce Mænad, even from the dim verge
Of the horizon to the zenith's height,
The locks of the approaching storm. Thou dirge

Of the dying year, to which this closing night
Will be the dome of a vast sepulchre,
Vaulted with all thy congregated might

Of vapours, from whose solid atmosphere
Black rain, and fire, and hail will burst: O hear!

III
Thou who didst waken from his summer dreams
The blue Mediterranean, where he lay,
Lull'd by the coil of his crystalline streams,

Beside a pumice isle in Baiæ's bay,
And saw in sleep old palaces and towers
Quivering within the wave's intenser day,

All overgrown with azure moss and flowers
So sweet, the sense faints picturing them! Thou
For whose path the Atlantic's level powers

Cleave themselves into chasms, while far below
The sea-blooms and the oozy woods which wear

The sapless foliage of the ocean, know

Thy voice, and suddenly grow gray with fear,
And tremble and despoil themselves: O hear!

IV
If I were a dead leaf thou mightest bear;
If I were a swift cloud to fly with thee;
A wave to pant beneath thy power, and share

The impulse of thy strength, only less free
Than thou, O uncontrollable! if even
I were as in my boyhood, and could be

The comrade of thy wanderings over heaven,
As then, when to outstrip thy skiey speed
Scarce seem'd a vision – I would ne'er have striven

As thus with thee in prayer in my sore need.
O! lift me as a wave, a leaf, a cloud!
I fall upon the thorns of life! I bleed!

A heavy weight of hours has chain'd and bow'd
One too like thee – tameless, and swift, and proud.

V
Make me thy lyre, even as the forest is:
What if my leaves are falling like its own?
The tumult of thy mighty harmonies

Will take from both a deep, autumnal tone,
Sweet though in sadness. Be thou, Spirit fierce,
My spirit! Be thou me, impetuous one!

Drive my dead thoughts over the universe,
Like wither'd leaves to quicken a new birth;
And, by the incantation of this verse,

Scatter, as from an unextinguish'd hearth
Ashes and sparks, my words among mankind!
Be through my lips to unawaken'd earth

The trumpet of a prophecy! O Wind,
If Winter comes, can Spring be far behind?

Percy Bysshe Shelley, 1820

Late September in Berlin and I'm a long way from the sea. I'm in bed reading about the local winds of Europe: the mistral, which blows north-westerly from southern France into the Mediterranean; the föhn, blowing warmly off the north side of the Alps. Then I find myself looking at weather forecasting websites back home in the UK. The surfer's site Magic Seaweed shows clever graphics of approaching winds and sea swells. The Orkney Harbours site gives readings taken from anemometers around the islands, on hilltops and piers. Sanday Weather provides detailed information about a single location on a small isle. I'm living far away but I keep coming back to these places, carried on the tides of the internet.

In the Orkney Islands at the north of Scotland, where there are very few trees, autumn is not much of a season. Summer quickly changes into the long winter, which blows in with the September equinox. Two years previously, I was home in Orkney at this time of year and spent a week challenging myself to swim in the sea every day. The nights before, I looked at the websites and planned where to go depending on the wind direction and height of tide. Because I was on an island, with coastline facing in all directions, I could always find a sheltered spot.

In the strongest winds, on days when it's too wild to swim, I try to walk into the gale. In a westerly storm on the island of Papay, I aim for the shoreline but my progress is slowed by sea spray, chunks of foam and grit being blown towards me. My eyes are watering, clothes and face being pulled backwards. The wind fills my ears and stirs my spirits, I feel in high pressure and held tightly. When I give up and turn around, I'm pushed by the wind into a run. I find it exciting but treat the coastline at these times with a healthy respect.

I download a tides app onto my phone. Here, I am able to see undulating graphs showing the movement between high and low tides at various points along the coast. It shows me their extent in metres, using data based on historical measurements. Inganess Bay is best to go to at low tide, when I can swim out as far as a shipwreck. High tide is better for swimming at Skipi Geo, when the sea comes up inside a cove. How the sea behaves around the islands, where the Atlantic meets the North Sea, is extremely complicated. Gaining this knowledge is a life's work for fishermen and ferry navigators.

On the autumn equinox, which falls around 23 September, day and night are the same length all over the globe, when the sun shines directly on the equator. 'Spring' tides, which take place twice a month, a few days after new and full moons, bring the highest and lowest water marks of the month. The sun, moon and earth are lined up, combining their gravitational pull on the oceans. The weeks around the equinoxes bring the biggest tidal ranges of the year for similar reasons. When the equinox coincides with spring tides, you get the largest tidal range of all. It is complex: another tidal cycle works itself out over 18.6 years. The distance of the moon, wind direction and air pressure also contribute.

It's at the equinox spring tides, at the very lowest waters, that people in Orkney are able to go out and hunt for spoots, the local name for razor clams, which live under the sand at the farthest reach of the beach. When I was a teenager, we picked winkles from the shore at low tide, scrambling on the slippy rocks and pools in the intertidal zone, and sold them by weight. On Radio Scotland, I heard a woman on the Isle of Harris say, 'If you want to do seaweed foraging, you've got to start consulting the moon.'

At the highest waters, the sea swells in the bays that edge Orkney. If spring tides are combined with an incoming wind, they can cause damage, erosion and flooding. In autumn 2013, ancient drystone walls on the island of North Ronaldsay, built to keep seaweed-eating sheep on the beach, tumbled down in such conditions.

I've only recently found out that these rhythms are in my family, my grandma telling me about how her father, a ship's supplier, had to go to work at high tide, shifts constantly changing. Mum has recently been learning about the tidal races and currents around Orkney with her kayak club. These cycles still affect people. Causeways to islands, the Churchill Barriers, are closed at certain high tides. I once unwittingly drove over the barriers at just the wrong time – high tide in an easterly wind – and my car was hit by a wave that breached the sea wall. I flicked on the windscreen wipers, held tightly to the wheel and drove on.

I'd long heard that as well as the biggest tides, the autumn equinox brings the strongest winds in Orkney. However, some say equinoctial gales are mostly anecdotal. Indeed, there is no straightforward mechanism that would relate the alignment of the planets to the areas of pressure that create wind. Reverend Charles Clouston, who began weather recording in Orkney in the nineteenth century, discovered that we don't actually get the strongest gales at the equinox but the idea still holds. An enquiry to my Orcadian friends on Facebook caused a debate.

Someone said that while we do get so-called equinoctial gales reliably in September and October, the windiest months are January and February. Another person maintained that despite science telling us it's all an old mariners' myth, with the change from Julian to Gregorian calendar meaning we're all out of kilter, she still thinks it is more windy around autumn equinox – and the spring one. She puts it down to the Norse god Njord bestirring himself.

The direction of the prevailing wind in Orkney, which may seem simple, also causes debate. It seems to depend on if you factor in strength and where you are standing. Some maintain the north wind is the most common. My dad, who farms on the west coast, reckons it is the westerlies. I'm told confidently that our extremes of wind are usually from the SW–NW quadrant. An environmental report from Orkney Islands Council says: 'The most characteristic feature of the Orkney climate is the frequency of strong winds and the prevailing winds are from between west and south-east for 60% of the year. Winds greater than 8 m s–1 occur for over 30% of the year and gales occur on average for 29 days per year.' I just know that when I'm away from Orkney and hear the wind outside my bedroom window, it makes me homesick.

It's pleasing to consider and observe celestial dynamics and see how the alignment of the earth, moon and sun can affect my plans: where to swim, when to forage on the seashore. I find it irresistible to tie these extremes of ocean and weather to my own life and moods. Henry David Thoreau wrote: 'The poet must be constantly watching his moods, as the astronomer watches the aspects of the heavens . . . A meteorological journal of the mind. You shall observe what occurs in your latitude, me mine.' An equinox sounds stable but really is an instant where the balance tips, and the nights become longer than days. It is the counterweight to the solstices.

Living in the city, the high winds and waters are something I experience as much digitally as physically. My electronic device links me to home and on the equinox I'm searching for a still point, something to hang on to in the hugeness of the internet, in the gales and the ever ebbing and flowing ocean.

Amy Liptrot, 2016

Autumn is an adventure, a season of transformation, and a time to prepare for the long winter ahead. It is a thousand leaves falling to the ground and nourishing the soil beneath; it is heavy rainfalls that catch you off guard and drive you to shelter; it is the refreshing winds that sweep the haze of summer away; it is the calm before the storm. More than that, though, autumn is a celebration of senses, of new experiences for your eyes, ears, tongue, skin and nose; it rouses your consciousness after the calming effects of summer. Autumn isn't the season of decay or death, but one of wealth and renewal. It is the changing landscape, the subtle anticipation of winter. Autumn is to be enjoyed.

Autumn is bold bursts of colour that leap from every corner of the landscape; it is golden yellow, fiery red, bright orange, and rich chocolate brown, and a faded green that reminds us of summer. It is an endless rolling landscape preparing itself for winter, the twinkling dew that clings to the cold grass and delicate spider webs, thick misty mornings and foggy evenings, and weak, watery sunlight that penetrates the skeletal trees. Autumn is a dappled night sky peppered with stars and clouds; it is a twinkle of sunlight captured in this morning's rainfall, or a day that ends too soon. Now is the time for the beauty of harvest; for all of the colours that burst from the hedgerows and trees. Autumn is blackberries, rosehips, elderberries, holly, rowanberries, conkers, acorns, sloe berries, pine and alder cones, hawthorns, and ivy; the joy of collecting such bountiful treasures. It is thick, sticky mud and the stains on your boots, the glow of a candle within a deep orange pumpkin, and the flurry of birds that come to feed in your garden. Stand bathed in the glow of a bonfire, and watch fireworks dance across a deep purple sky.

Autumn is the scent of wet pavements, and the perfume of damp leaves as they lie trodden into the ground. It is the season of crackling bonfires, fireworks, and harvest; the aroma of a hundred fireworks' smoky trails, disturbed embers, and intoxicating bouquets from recently ploughed fields. Autumn is the scent of a farmhouse kitchen; of fresh bread, newly baked plum pie, roasted chestnuts, and the sweet cologne of an over-flowing fruit bowl. It is the earthy tones of a recently carved pumpkin, the sweet tang of stewing apples, and the inviting odours of Christmas preparation. Autumn brings the fragrant rain; heavy, fat drops that cleanse everything that they touch. It is the season of renewal, when every breath invokes nature.

Autumn is the crunch of leaves as they scatter underfoot; it's the rustles, rattles, and whispers of a woodland walk, and the wind whipping through bare branches and heaped foliage. It is the whistle of fireworks, and the crackle and pop as they burst into life; it's the sputter and roar of a bonfire, a warning to keep your distance. Autumn is the season of squeals and giggles, and of laughter from painted faces.

Listen: silence hides a multitude of creatures. Autumn is the snuffle of hedgehogs as they creep through the grass, the twitter of birds as they come home to roost, the honk of geese as they seek warmer climes. It's nature's orchestra performing at its very best; every inch of the landscape strives to be heard. Autumn is the rain as it plops on the ground, drips into big metal buckets and soaks into the earth. It's the cacophony of rainfall on a tin shed roof, the patter of streams as they form on the ground, and the gush of a woodland waterfall. Autumn is a playground filling with conkers that clash together; it's leaf piles that have been disturbed by wellington-clad feet, the squelch of mud, and the trudging of feet on wet ground. It is the ooze of wet leaves between your fingers; of mud between your toes. It's the chill of the rain as it dampens your skin, the cold, crisp air, and the roughness of the wind as it whips your cheeks. Step outside and embrace the chill in the air; autumn is the soft comfort of a warm woolly hat, the feel of a scarf as it slides around your neck, and the heat from a new pair of gloves. Now is the time for droplets of dew to form in the thick grass; ripple your fingers through the moist stems, and catch the beads as they drip and fall. Autumn is the heat of a roaring bonfire, the scold of stray ash, and the smothering curtain of smoke that envelops you; it's the fizz of sparklers clenched in cold fists; the warmth of your breath as it escapes your lips. Autumn is damp socks after a long walk, crusts of mud that crack and crumble, and splashes that rain down after a satisfying puddle jump. It's the roughness of logs as you arrange a home for a hibernating hedgehog, the prickle of a conker not yet out of its casing, the coarse edges of pine and alder cones collected by children. Autumn is a time for textured treasure; run your fingers through its landscape.

Louise Baker, 2016

The Autumnal Season sets in about Michaelmas with cooler air, often cold nights, but for the most part fine weather; as it advances, and the temperature continues to decline, it frequently produces showers and wet weather, accompanied with high gales of wind which prevail most during the night, and are often succeeded by dead calms in the day time. Fogs begin to become denser and to last all day, overspreading the meadows to great extent in low and flat situations, and not being overcome even by the sun's midday rays; Phoebus cannot say of himself as he did in Ovid's time

'Qui modo pestifero tot jugera ventre prementem, Stravimus innumeris tumidum Pythona sagittis.'

About Allhallowtide in the neighbourhood of London and of Amsterdam the faint beams of the sun are hardly seen for two hours in twenty four, and this for many days together. Occasionally fogs happen at every period of the autumn and winter, but this is the season of their prevalence.

The retreat of the Swallows and Martlets constitutes one of the most remarkable features in the history of this period. Swallows assemble early in September, and so continue to appear in vast quantities, roosting on the tops of houses and lofty buildings; their migration begins with the Autumnal Season, and the greatest part of the species migrate between new and old Michaelmas day; Martlets retire a few days later; straggling Swallows are seen about till the middle of October, and Martlets sometimes till the end of that month. Many birds now arrive in flocks; wild Geese and Ducks perform partial migrations, and Woodcocks and Snipes arrive. The flowering of the Saffrons, the autumnal Crocus, the purple and the white varieties of the Colchicum in our gardens, Michaelmas Daisies, and other late Asters, are indications of the approach of this season. Fungi now become very abundant in moist places.

The leaves during the Autumnal Season turn yellow, red, or brown, and at length falling, by degrees cover the ground with thick carpeting. The Beech, the Oak, and few deciduous trees keep their old dead leaves till spring.

A colder air, wet fogs, or alternations of wind and fine weather, close this period at the end of November.

Thomas Furly Forster, The Pocket Encyclopaedia of Natural Phenomena, *published 1827*

It is the month of ripeness – a golden, crimson and russet month. Here in Kent the orchards offer themselves to stage the drama of the year. Throughout the summer, when the fields around were alive with the sounds of haymaking and harvest, these miles of trees grew in silence, while the pale green of the swelling apples hid beneath the leaves. Since their pink and white foaming in May, no one has remarked them, except perhaps the mower as he cut the grass from around their feet, or the farmer as he has watched the apples setting. But now all that is changed. These calm golden days have brought ladders and shouting, the creaking of wheels and the thud of falling apples.

The gatherers come early, when the dew on the heavy grass and nettles wets their legs and bediamonds the leaves, and there is a mysterious gloom and depth of shadow along the aisles of trees.

A glow burns through the countryside at the thought of the apple gathering. 'They have started picking,' say the old people to each other down in the village. Something stirs in their blood, a memory of gatherings when the mistletoe was sacred, and prayer gave motion to the sun, and stones were still alive. So, too, do their hands and minds leap mountains and centuries, linking in pagan continuity with gods, grape-stained in their Mediterranean vineyards. It is one of the pinnacles in the rhythm of their year.

The army of ladders attacks the trees. On all sides, at all

angles, are they reared, placed against unresisting branches and in the clefts of gnarled trunks – a veritable fugue in ladders. The old men with their baskets on a hook start picking the lower apples within reach of the safety of the ground; rheumaticky limbs are not so fond of climbing. But the youth leap the ladders, and systematically the pillage begins. The trees shake and tremble, the figures run up and down, emptying picking aprons, exchanging full for empty baskets; and the branches leap upwards, relieved of their weight of fruit.

And now the sun is high and each tree courteously spreads a circular dark green carpet of shade beneath itself. They stretch, these circles of shadows, back into the shapelessness of distance, narrowing into ellipses as they go.

At midday, as the sun beats down upon the browned arms of the pickers, the men step with relief into the shade. It is dinner time. Bottles of cold tea and beer are produced, and chunks of cheese and bread; and leaning against the trunks of the trees they sit, or sprawling in the shadow, they eat and talk. Old Tom Latimer has picked 'this seventy year'. He mumbles with his toothless jaw, comparing this tree with that, this year's yield with the one of thirty years back. He is himself like one of his own apples; red lacquer stains each cheek, wizened as an apple forgotten in the loft. As a shepherd knows each sheep in his flock, so is the intimate shape of each apple tree stamped upon Tom's mind. He shakes his head at the young men lazing, and is off up the ladders again.

So throughout the hot afternoon they pick, moving their ladders and baskets over the board of the orchard like counters in a game. And as the pickers move, they are followed by the clumps of men who sort the apples. Instinctively, mechanically, they select them, by weight and soundness, dealing them out into the right bushel baskets. Following the group of baskets, in their turn come the carts. There is a swishing sound as they brush the trees in passing. The horse tosses his head into the lower leaves of the tree, against the attacking flies. And so the fruit of the trees is taken away, to be covered up and labelled and put into a railway siding, for grey-faced people in the cities who never saw an apple shine upon the top-most bough against the blue of the September sky.

But what is that shouting away over the fields? What is that music of mouth organ and concertina? Beyond the trees and past the next slope ends another harvesting and the ravaged Kentish hop fields are lying back to rest. While still the apple trees bent beneath their fruit, these hop fields were half stripped. Poles were torn up, wreathed with the tendrilled hop plants, and laid against the canvas tally baskets, till they looked like the oars of an ancient galley. Here, for the picking, gather the outpourings of the London slums, in all their flimsy finery and their fear of rain, cumbered with babies and tin tea kettles. The fields must have shivered with the clamour. Girl shouted to girl across the avenues of hop poles; old woman quarrelled with old woman, till the feathers in their bonnets nodded drunkenly; sun-cheated children chased each other among the tally baskets; tired, white-faced men sighed from out their contentment as they counted the diminishing days before they should be sent back to the heaving heat of the London pavements. And over it all was the beauty of the hop plants, like a blessing.

But with cheers and shouting, concertinas and song, the last lorry load of pickers has left the hop fields, and the naked hop poles stand silent.

Over the country there is peace. The resting fields have given up their yield. Oast houses and rickyards and barns are full. In the cottage gardens the fruit has been picked, apple and pear, quince and plum. Go down the village street on a late September afternoon and the warm burnt smell of jam-making oozes out of open cottage doors. Soon the last apple will have been picked and the orchards will be silent again.

Sunday evening in the village church: the days are drawing in and the smelly gas lamps flicker unevenly with the greenish yellow light. It is Harvest Festival and the church is full. Farmer Stevens peeps behind him to look with a sense of possession at his sheaves of wheat around the font. Old Mrs Yeo is wondering where her orange dahlias have been put, and knows that the pink ones in the place of honour on the pulpit are not as good as hers. Rows of large apples line the chancel, red and yellow and green. The lectern is almost hidden in a tangle of oats. Obscurely at the back sits a ploughboy. He is shy and fidgets with his bow under the unaccustomed constriction of his Sunday collar. He has lost his way in the Service, for he never comes to church. But every year the Harvest Festival pulls him. He listens to the vicar preaching; he sees the squire and his lady in the front pew, and all the gentry smiling to each other. He feels lonely and untidy. Suddenly a flame of understanding consumes him. He is surrounded by white light and God's hand is upon him. This is *his* service. It is about *him* that the vicar is preaching. He no longer fears the squire and his lady and all the gentry in the church. Those oats are his, and the wheat round the font. Who but he knew the fields before the plough had turned them? Was it not he who rose in the dark of winter mornings and with chilblained hands and numb feet fed the horses? Who else but he had withstood the March gales as he followed the plough? And now it is Harvest Festival. He strains forward to look at the apples, the oats and the wheat.

'Yes,' he tells himself. 'It is mine! All mine.'

To the ploughboy the meaning of gathering is revealed.

Clare Leighton, The Farmer's Year:
A Calendar of English Husbandry, *1933*

Tithonus

The woods decay, the woods decay and fall,
The vapours weep their burthen to the ground,
Man comes and tills the field and lies beneath,
And after many a summer dies the swan.
Me only cruel immortality
Consumes: I wither slowly in thine arms,
Here at the quiet limit of the world,
A white-hair'd shadow roaming like a dream
The ever-silent spaces of the East,
Far-folded mists, and gleaming halls of morn.

  Alas! for this gray shadow, once a man –
So glorious in his beauty and thy choice,
Who madest him thy chosen, that he seem'd
To his great heart none other than a God!
I ask'd thee, 'Give me immortality.'
Then didst thou grant mine asking with a smile,
Like wealthy men, who care not how they give.
But thy strong Hours indignant work'd their wills,
And beat me down and marr'd and wasted me,
And tho' they could not end me, left me maim'd
To dwell in presence of immortal youth,
Immortal age beside immortal youth,
And all I was, in ashes. Can thy love,

Thy beauty, make amends, tho' even now,
Close over us, the silver star, thy guide,
Shines in those tremulous eyes that fill with tears
To hear me? Let me go: take back thy gift:
Why should a man desire in any way
To vary from the kindly race of men
Or pass beyond the goal of ordinance
Where all should pause, as is most meet for all?

A soft air fans the cloud apart; there comes
A glimpse of that dark world where I was born.
Once more the old mysterious glimmer steals
From thy pure brows, and from thy shoulders pure,
And bosom beating with a heart renew'd.
Thy cheek begins to redden thro' the gloom,
Thy sweet eyes brighten slowly close to mine,
Ere yet they blind the stars, and the wild team
Which love thee, yearning for thy yoke, arise,
And shake the darkness from their loosen'd manes,
And beat the twilight into flakes of fire.

Lo! ever thus thou growest beautiful
In silence, then before thine answer given
Departest, and thy tears are on my cheek.

Why wilt thou ever scare me with thy tears,
And make me tremble lest a saying learnt,
In days far-off, on that dark earth, be true?
'The Gods themselves cannot recall their gifts.'

Ay me! ay me! with what another heart
In days far-off, and with what other eyes
I used to watch – if I be he that watch'd –
The lucid outline forming round thee; saw
The dim curls kindle into sunny rings;
Changed with thy mystic change, and felt my blood
Glow with the glow that slowly crimson'd all
Thy presence and thy portals, while I lay,
Mouth, forehead, eyelids, growing dewy-warm
With kisses balmier than half-opening buds
Of April, and could hear the lips that kiss'd
Whispering I knew not what of wild and sweet,
Like that strange song I heard Apollo sing,
While Ilion like a mist rose into towers.

Yet hold me not for ever in thine East:
How can my nature longer mix with thine?
Coldly thy rosy shadows bathe me, cold
Are all thy lights, and cold my wrinkled feet
Upon thy glimmering thresholds, when the steam
Floats up from those dim fields about the homes
Of happy men that have the power to die,
And grassy barrows of the happier dead.
Release me, and restore me to the ground;
Thou seëst all things, thou wilt see my grave:
Thou wilt renew thy beauty morn by morn;
I earth in earth forget these empty courts,
And thee returning on thy silver wheels.

Alfred, Lord Tennyson, 1860

Every day in autumn I am drawn to St John's Point's black-and-yellow-striped lighthouse, the tallest in Ireland, to immerse myself in the solitude of nature, to listen out for birds and to look out to sea. Above the rhythm of breaking waves the seven whistles of a whimbrel might be all I hear, or the shrill 'kleep' of an oystercatcher. Little else. What peace! I like it most when a strong wind is blowing onshore, preferably from the southeast and accompanied by squalls and poor visibility. On such days I might stay out all day, my black lab Django by my side. The idea of staring through a telescope for an insane number of hours on an exposed headland does not have wide appeal – I'm usually seawatching alone, or with my son, Tim. For us, seawatching is a drug. The worse the weather the better: gale force winds and rain, yes please!

Few parts of the world can match the British Isles for the richness of seabirds that gather each summer to breed on its bountiful islands and isolated rocks, or pass offshore each autumn, sometimes in spectacular numbers. Of the twenty-five regularly breeding seabirds in Great Britain and Ireland all but two, Leach's petrel and little tern, regularly pass St John's Point. Often, all that the casual observer needs is a pair of binoculars to marvel at a constant stream of seabirds of a dozen or so species. Red-throated diver, gannet, kittiwake, razorbill and Manx shearwater are some of the point's staple species, while black-throated diver, Sabine's gull and storm petrel can provide the icing on a really good seawatch. Thousands of auks, gulls and terns commute between the open sea and fish-rich shallows of Dundrum Bay, while more pelagic species such as skuas will enter the bay in pursuit of food or temporary respite before resuming their course.

One bird, above all, is symbolic of the Celtic seas: the magical Manx shearwater. Mesmerising in its flight, alternating black above and white below, the Manx shearwater effortlessly banks from side to side, rising and falling on its long slim wings, masterfully freewheeling through peaks and troughs; sometimes, when travelling between breeding and fishing grounds or on migration, for hundreds of miles at a time. It has no fear of the sea. Coming to land, which the adult birds must do in order to breed, is another thing. With set back legs designed for swimming not walking, shearwaters are easy meat for predatory gulls and their kin. Which is why they only come ashore under the cover of darkness. Some days there are many more Manxies passing St John's Point than the 10,000 that breed nearby on Lighthouse Island, which is one of the three Copeland isles that lie just outside the mouth of Belfast Lough. So it must be assumed that birds are being drawn from the much bigger colonies to the north and south: Rum in Scotland and Skomer, Skokholm and Middleholm in Wales, which between them account for 80 per cent of the world population of c. 370,000 pairs. The scientific name, *Puffinus puffinus*, comes from *puffin*, originally meaning the cured carcass of the nestling shearwater but later, confusingly, also that of the unrelated puffin. The common name originates from the Calf of Man – visible from St John's Point – where possibly the largest colony of all once existed, though few breed there now.

Manx shearwaters, like most seabirds, are long-lived. Scientists at Copeland Bird Observatory have been monitoring the colony of Manxies since the observatory's foundation seventy years ago. One shearwater ringed in the 1950s was more than fifty years old when last observed. Another, caught and ringed on Bardsey Island in 1957 as a breeding adult – so already at least five years old – was subsequently caught on four more occasions, most recently in 2003, confirming it as one of the oldest recorded birds ever. During their half-century of annual journeys to and from wintering areas off the coast of Brazil and Argentina they are estimated to have flown 5 million miles (8,045,000 km) – more than ten times to the Moon and back.

Raising a Manx shearwater chick is a lengthy affair, spanning almost four months. For the first two months after hatching one of the parents remains with their single offspring in the burrow while the other goes out to sea, returning after several days with a full crop of partly digested small fish and squid. The chick is literally fattened up over the next few weeks, with both parents bringing food. The young bird then remains alone in its burrow for a further eight to nine days before it embarks on its maiden flight entirely unaccompanied – quite an adventure after having lived underground until then. Manx shearwaters lead exciting lives: after the exhausting business of breeding it appears they like to party, spending the winter in the coastal waters of South America: Copeland to Copacabana! Their return migration, beginning in March, carries them northward across the Equator to the Caribbean, where they pick up the Gulf Stream and head out over the North Atlantic, arriving at their Celtic island sanctuaries from mid-April onward. At St John's Point Tim and I will be waiting to welcome them home.

Chris Murphy, 2016

Fall of the Leaf. The decay and fall of the foliage is a phenomenon which takes place during the autumnal season, beginning with the early trees, as limes, elms, and others about Michaelmas, and continuing till the feast of St. Catherine, Nov. 25th, after which few leaves are left except on the oaks, and some trees which scarcely shed them at all till spring.

Thomas Furly Forster, The Pocket Encyclopaedia
of Natural Phenomena, *published 1827*

There is a sorrow to September, a space left in the sky by the swifts. Plants and grasses, gold with summer's sun, are tousled now by the first of autumn's storms. Even September's songsters speak of sadness. Silent since the spring, the robins start again their tragic trickle of a song, telling of winter's coming. From the autumn-tangled stands of bramble come the introspective chirps of dark bush-crickets. 'The crickets felt it was their duty to warn everyone that summertime cannot last forever. Even on the most beautiful days in the whole year – the days when summer is changing into fall – the crickets spread the rumour of sadness and change.' So wrote E. B. White in *Charlotte's Web*.

Change, though, is a certainty if you live on a planet with a tilted axis in respect to its source of heat and light. After the giddy upswing of May and the fat abundance of July and August must inevitably – so the heavens have it – come the sadness, the sense of loss of September; as leaves curl and yellow, as summer's migrants wink out one by one, and as the blackberries turn to tasteless pap.

There's little point in being human, however, if you can't embrace a magnificent melancholy. Just as seasons go with a tilted planetary axis, melancholy goes with humanity, and September is its month. On a damp, storm-wracked day – the day on which the leaden sadness of the end of summer grasps your heart – walk a wild beach in North Norfolk. Crunch across the deep line of razorshells, witnesses to the astounding productivity of the Wash, and kick the sullen sand with the toes of your boots. To sea, the Sandwich terns are gathering, froth-white against the hammered pewter of the water. With them is their nemesis, the dark dart of an arctic skua, fresh from the tundra with piracy in its eyes. It chases the hapless terns until, worn out, they drop the fish they've caught into its thieving bill. Even the Sandwich terns know September's sadness.

Inland the sorrow hangs heavy like an autumn mist. The straggling clematis has flowered and gone to silky seed; the cast of butterflies – spring's skippers, summer's blues and hairstreaks – all have flown and died; even the oaks have mildewed in the damp. Yet even as winter's dark and cold and damp are presaged by the yellowing, dying vegetation all around, you spot a fresh little violet flower on a chalky bank. An autumn gentian, peeking bravely into bloom as all else fades.

September is a melancholy month, but as Henry David Thoreau wrote, 'The doctrine of despair was never taught by such as shared the serenity of nature.' In an autumn gentian's little flower is another spring foretold.

Nick Acheson, 2014

It feels as if it's been raining for weeks. As I stare out over the garden all I can see is a lake of bouncing water. Only a month ago the freshly hatched and mated queen bumblebees were busy feeding in the meadow and I was lying next to them with the warm buzz of late summer around me. Now I can't see a single living creature and I hope the bumbles are hibernating deep in the mound of autumn leaves I've piled up behind the shed. It's grey, depressing and wet – autumn has arrived and, to be honest, it's not living up to its golden reputation.

As I go to bed I can still hear the rain beating on the window. That's unusual, as the roof overhang usually stops the rain from touching the glass, but this is rain with attitude, wind-driven horizontal rain, and as I slide under the duvet and close my eyes I try to block out the weather outside. That's when I notice the scratching.

At first I try to kid myself that it's a twig rubbing against the window, but the longer it goes on, the longer my brain seems to tune into its persistent rhythm and I can't get away from the fact that it's coming from the attic. As I eventually drift off to sleep, rats the size of small dogs and giant marauding grey squirrels fill my dreams and I'm quite surprised to wake to thin watery sunshine and total silence.

The next morning I'm unceremoniously nominated to 'investigate' the sounds by my husband, and as I climb the ladder and push open the hatch I'm actually a bit disappointed when everything in the attic seems totally normal. I wander around for a while, stub my toe on a suitcase in the dim orange light from the swinging fluorescent tube, and wish I was wearing more than just my dressing gown. Then I spot them: unmistakable tiny black mouse droppings, smaller than a grain of rice, perched precariously on top of the box with 'Christmas decorations' scrawled on its side. Sleuthing concludes for the day.

By the next day I've managed to convince myself there's probably just one mouse who's probably been flooded out of his garden home. In autumn, as the weather grows cold and wet, it's not unknown for rural woodmice to take sanctuary in our dry, warm homes. I need to trap and release it – killing isn't an option in my book. I get on the phone to a friend at a local Wildlife Trust and ask if I can please borrow a few Longworth small mammal traps. I've used these before to help survey a local nature reserve for small mammals. They look like little metal tunnels with a bigger box on the end, and the mouse, vole or shrew wanders in (tempted by some tasty morsels and bedding already in the larger box compartment) and as it moves over a small trip mechanism the door to the tunnel falls shut behind it. The mammal is safe, will have plenty of food and will be quite comfortable until I can release it a few hours later – perfect. The Wildlife Trust agree to let me borrow a few.

That night I set up six traps between the suitcases, boxes and discarded gym equipment in the attic. In the morning four out of six doors are closed. It seems I might have slightly underestimated the extent of the mouse migration. I carefully place the first trap into a deep see-through plastic bag and as I take the trap apart the contents gently wriggle into the bag. I quickly remove the trap, hold the bag shut and lift it to eye level. I come face to face with twitchy-nosed woodmouse number one.

There's no getting away from the fact that woodmice are cute. With enormous black eyes and long whiskers it stares back at me through the plastic bag. I've decided to release it under the shed, where it should be dry and safe. I hurry down the ladder, down the stairs, out of the back door, down the garden, round the back of the shed and within seconds it's free and hopping like a tiny brown kangaroo over a couple of twigs before diving for cover. Half an hour later I've successfully re-located the other three. Job done.

That night the scratching from the attic is worse than ever.

OK. There's obviously quite a big family up there. I set all six traps the next night, and four more are closed in the morning. That's now eight woodmice I've trapped. I repeat the release procedure and tell myself that surely that must be it?

That night I not only hear scratching, but scampering and squeaks too.

I set all six traps again and the next morning five are shut. We're now up to unlucky-for-some thirteen and I'm beginning to get worried. The attic must be overrun with woodmice – and yet there's hardly any sign of them. I can't quite under-stand what's going on, so I take to the internet in the hope of finding some answers.

Did you know woodmice have amazing homing instincts? I didn't. After two further days of marking each mouse caught with a dab of animal friendly coloured marker on the back of its neck, and catching the same five marked mice two nights in a row, I realise that a little journey in the car might be necessary if I am ever going to stop these persistent five from returning to the attic. On the third morning I drove the little wood-mouse family three miles down the road and released them together into a beautiful ancient wood with plenty of mouse hidey-holes.

It's now a week later and I'm lying in bed. It's perfectly quiet. The scratching, scampering and squeaking has stopped. They haven't returned . . . yet.

Jane Adams, 2016

October

Oct. 1.   Wheat out at Buriton, Froxfield, Ropley, & other places.

Oct. 2.   Flying ants, male & female, usually swarm, & migrate on hot sunny days in August & September; but this day a vast emigration took place in my garden, & myriads came forth in appearance, from the drain which goes under the fruit-wall; filling the air & the adjoining trees & shrubs with their numbers. The females were full of eggs. This late swarming is probably owing to the backward, wet season. The day following, not one flying ant was to be seen. The males, it is supposed all perish: the females wander away; & such as escape from Hirundines get into the grass, & under stones, & tiles, & lay the foundation of future colonies.

Oct. 3.   Hirundines swarm around the Plestor, & up & down the street.

Oct. 6.   Many Hirundines: several very young swallows on the thatch of the cottage near the pound. The evening is uncommonly dark.

Oct. 7.   The crop of stoneless berberries is prodigious! Among the many sorts of people that are injured by this very wet summer, the peat-cutters are great sufferers: for they have not disposed of half the peat

& turf which they have prepared; & the poor have lost their season for laying in their forest-fuel. The brick-burner can get no dry heath to burn his lime, & bricks: nor can I house my cleft wood, which lies drenched in wet. The brick-burner could never get his last makings of tiles & bricks dry enough for burning the autumn thro'; so they must be destroyed, & worked up again. He had paid duty for them; but is, as I understand, to be reimbursed.

Oct. 9.   Maser Hale houses barley that looks like old thatch. Much barley about the country, & some wheat. Some pheasants found in the manour. The sound of great guns was heard distinctly this day to the S. E. probably from Goodwood, where the Duke of Richmond has a detachment from the train of artillery encamped in his park, that he may try experiments with some of the ordnance.

Oct. 11.   Dr Chandler mows the church-litten closes for hay. Farmer Parsons houses pease, which have been hacked for weeks. Barley abroad.

Oct. 12.   Gathered in the dearling apples: fruit small, & stunted.

Oct. 19.   Made presents of berberries to several neighbours. Ring-ouzel seen in the Kings field.

Oct. 23.   Dr Bingham & family left Selborne.

Oct. 26.   Hired two old labourers to house my cleft billet wood, which is still in a damp, cold condition, & should have been under cover some months ago, had the weather permitted.

Oct. 27.   Some few grapes just eatable: a large crop. Housed all the billet wood. Leaves fall in showers. A curlew is heard loudly whistling on the hill towards the Wadden. On this day, Mrs S. Barker was brought to bed of a boy, who advances my nepotes to the round & compleat number of 60.

Oct. 28. Thomas saw a polecat run across the garden.

Oct. 29. Finished piling my wood: housed the bavins: fallows very wet.

Oct. 30. Planted 100 of cabbages, in ground well dunged, to stand the winter.

Reverend Gilbert White, The Naturalist's Journal, *1792*

The October sky is bright, with a glowing film of city vapour. I live in a smoke-filled bubble, encircled by the M25. It's a wonder anything survives here, let alone a nature junkie like me.

I push my way past Caribbean hairdressers and food-and-wine shops to a spot around the corner that's usually good for what ails me. The woods nearest (and dearest) to me are on a steep hill – though the view from the top makes up for the muddy climb.

As the tarmac underfoot turns to earth I breathe a sigh of relief. The silence seems overwhelming. Just seconds ago I was in a concrete jungle, but now I stand surrounded by damp earth, wood and October's sepia tones. I'm still in an urban bubble, but the air here seems clearer somehow.

Summer's warmth has long since left the wood and I'm beginning to wish I'd brought my coat. Fallen leaves crunch satisfyingly underfoot like breakfast cereal. I head into the undergrowth, the tang of leaf mould on my tongue. This secret woodland is always deserted. On an old wooden post an arrow points right, although I'm not sure what it's directing me to. As far as I can tell I'm lost in the wild, just as I want to be.

With a screeching 'ki-ki-ki', I'm no longer alone. The trees shake as dozens of neon-green parakeets sound their alarms. Cover blown, I stand and wait as the frenzy of beating wings quietens down to a simmer. This is their turf, and I'm an intruder. These woods, like many others in London, are home to rose-ringed parakeets (*Psittacula krameri*), and it feels as though this is their stronghold, the place they return to once all the cherry trees and bird feeders in the nearby gardens have been stripped bare. It's hard not to love these garish invaders with their clown-like beaks and bold personalities. As I turn to walk away from their circus, one pops its head out of a hole to look at me with perfect comic timing.

I take a detour via one of the wood's barely used tracks. A speck shoots past me into the bracken: *firecrest*! The flash of orange on its forehead is the only way of telling it apart from its cousin, the goldcrest. These autumn featherweights are a highlight of the season. Due to their camouflage of yellow and orange, spotting one seems less likely than finding a needle in the proverbial haystack. Britain's smallest bird is not, however, lacking in character – and likes to make itself known. Spending most of their time upside down as they flit from branch to branch, they are nature's trapeze artists.

At the top of the wood, in a clearing, stands one of South London's iconic antennae. For something so massive and un-natural to be in the woodland feels jarring, but the birds don't mind it at all; in fact several parakeets perch on its frame to enjoy the same view for which I've traipsed through mud and dead leaves.

Having reached this vantage point I choose the least woodlouse-riddled log I can find and sit for a while. I love these city woods. Most are low-lying, with views no more than fifty feet in front, but here I can see for miles. Evergreens stick out through the mosaic of coppery deciduous foliage and brown earth. This is where the change in seasons can be best appreciated.

AUTUMN

When I think of the woods, I think of autumn, for woods are nature's calendar. No other landscape is transformed so totally, and none more dramatically than by the annual autumn gilding. With the sepia tones comes an almost overwhelming sense of nostalgia. I'm cast back to my childhood, building dens and collecting pine cones. I was brought up a nature junkie – and I've found my fix, here in the heart of the city.

Will Harper-Penrose, 2016

I have been driving my little motorhome to the northwest of Scotland for ever and the silence when the engine's switched off is almost shocking. There is no sound at all through the van's open window. No traffic, no sirens, no service station cacophony. I let out my breath as if I've been holding it all journey long.

After bumping along a track off a minor road across Rannoch Moor I'm at my first wild camping spot. I need to stretch, to breathe some clean moorland air, to just let go ... let the impact on my senses soften the hard concentration of a day's driving. I've been so windscreen-focused for the last hundred miles or so that the patchwork of autumn colours in the densely wooded Trossachs and the bedspreads of heathers beyond scarcely got a glance. I get out and look properly at the vast sweeping curves of moor and mountain surrounding me.

It's early October, before the clocks go back, so although it's evening, there's still some dusky light glowing in the western sky, turning the pinks and mauves of heather to deep purple. A distant lochan is navy blue. The view soothes and enfolds me.

I stretch out my chest, arms and hands, put my head back and breathe in lungfuls of heather fragrance, dampness, a luscious earthiness. I feel like a wild animal newly released from captivity. Listening intently, there's only the sound of a stream and the call of a distant bird of prey. I love this season in all its manifestations, but such a fresh, scented, darkening evening must be the best ever autumnal experience.

Then, not far behind me, comes the sound of a cow making the strangest bellowing noise. I'm nervous around cows in general, and this particular one sounds in pain. I hadn't seen any cows on the moor, or even suitable pasture for them, so I turn around, searching.

The 'cow' is a magnificent red deer stag. He is, thankfully, further away than expected: the depth and volume of his rutting roar made it sound as if he was much closer. I can hardly believe it: the stag is a complete Monarch of the Glen cliché. He's facing the same way as the painting, his head similarly angled to the right, and with the same shaped hills in the background. His antler rack looks identical too, and when seen through my binoculars, there's even a small hillock with a tuft of vegetation to his left, as in Landseer's original oil painting. He has the same thick, russety-brown neck mane.

I am rooted to the ground, and he, fortunately, is unmoving too, though through the binoculars I can see his nostrils pulsing, and his massive chest lifting. As he raises his head and blasts out another roar, I suddenly become un-rooted, and head for the van, quivering with excitement and fear. Time to put the kettle on. Drinking tea and eating cheese and biscuits – too excited to bother with cooking – I keep checking through the van's open door, but soon I can no longer see, or hear him, or anything other than the tumbling stream. The show is over; it's time to make up my bed.

Before settling down I step out into the night. A gibbous moon is rising in the eastern sky, and there are still a few sparse ribbons of light in the west. No stag noises, though there are tiny rustlings in the heather which make me almost as nervous. It will only be a mouse, or something similar, but in my imagination it's a woman-eating Highland Black Panther. I love being outdoors at night, yet some primal fear always makes me want to head back to the cave. But it's genuine tiredness too, and my sleeping bag calls.

I have a wonderful dream. I'm autumn personified, fearlessly dancing inside a circle of glistening red fly agaric, watched by badgers, foxes, hares and other smaller creatures. I am an androgynous hybrid with the head of a stag, antlers threaded through with mossy fronds and autumn berries, yet I have a curvaceous woman's body dressed in a diaphanous heather-coloured silk. Beyond the circle, rutting stags are parallel walking. The largest raises his head and roars . . . I wake up with a shock to an undreamlike stereophonic roaring, and scramble to the window.

The moon is fully risen and flooding the moorland landscape with a sharp, silver light. In the distance, a group of hinds feeding. And here, right next to the van, is the Monarch . . . I'm sure it's him. The window is open a fraction, and his smell floods into the van: it's like nothing I've ever experienced before. Rich, peaty, ammonic, atavistic: perhaps it's still the dream.

But then I understand why the stereo effect: another stag roars from a short distance away, and Monarch responds. His sound is as deep and rich as his smell and so loud that the side of the van reverberates against my shoulder. Even in the safety of this metal box cave, I feel afraid. He moves around the front of the van and I watch, and wait.

I was too tired earlier to put up my front windscreen cover, so now I can see him checking out the opposition. Although the other stag is further away, in the bright moonlight I can see it's smaller than Monarch, and has fewer tines. One more van-shaking roar from Monarch, and the upstart turns away. After a brief bout of pawing the ground Monarch moves towards his females, his smell lingering on the night air.

I watch the group for a while, but there is only a little sniffing of the females by Monarch, and soon they move off into the darkness. Clouds begin to cover the moon, so this time it's the dark night which spreads out across the sky as I return to my sleeping bag and my dreams.

Daphne Pleace, 2016

On Monday evening, October 1st, the visitors slowly concentrated themselves at the Speech House, in the Forest of Dean, and were met on the following morning in the Forest, or afterwards at the Hotel, by the Hereford contingent. Cold it might be, for some of the party swept the snow from the grass into their hands at about 10 a.m.: but it was clear and bright. As for the fungi, truly they were few and far between, the oldest excursionist venturing the opinion that it was the worst prospect of a fungus foray which the Woolhope Club ever experienced, bad as it was in the previous year. The ground was moist enough, it is true, but so cold, that only on the sunniest slopes could the commonest species be found, and even these were scarce and scattered. Whether in anticipation of such a result, or from a combination of various circumstances, the company was much smaller than usual. [. . .]

No record was kept of the species observed, but nearly everything in moderately good condition found its way into the collecting baskets, and yet they were not full. Rarities and novelties were out of the question, and never, perhaps, were common species treated with so much care and consideration. Even *Agaricus mellcus* and *A. fascicularis* were treated with respect; one gentle-man actually took off his hat in the presence of almost the only specimen of *A. rubescens* encountered in the Forest. Last year *Cantharellus aurantiacus* was one of the commonest species, sometimes growing by hundreds, but this year not a single one could be found. There was no dearth of walking

– naught but walking 'on, on, for ever' – to stoop and pick up a fungus was an event, but, alas! it was seldom worth the trouble of stooping for. It was worthy of note, that although the large genus *Agaricus* contains some 700 British species, the number seen was singularly few, the proportion being very far less than in most other genera, whilst, in the number of individuals, *Lactarius* and *Russula* exceeded it. *Coprinus* was seen but once or twice, and all the species of *Cortinarius* were extremely rare. Dinner at the Speech House Hotel, and a careful scrutiny of all the baskets, with the inevitable 'nightcaps', ended the first day.

On the Wednesday the members proceeded by train to Park End, which proved so satisfactory last year; but here again they were doomed to disappointment, for although more prolific than any spot visited on the Tuesday, yet the best was very bad, nothing of interest being found except some very fine specimens of *Russula inteora*, and a few *Hiigrophori*. Strolling slowly back through devious ways to Speech House, soon after two o'clock, light refreshment and waggonettes carried the party a drive of eight miles to Newnham Station for Hereford, and completed the two memorable days of fungus hunting in the Forest of Dean. Like bears of the forest, in another corner of Europe, the fungi had retreated to the mountains, and would not be found.

Woolhope Naturalists' Field Club, 1887

Yellow alder, russet beech and sessile oak; broadleaf trees stand guard over the stream in this steep-sided Welsh valley. Sunbeams pierce a rising mist, hinting at the winter chills to come. A high amber ridge-line is just visible through the canopy, raised against a gun-metal sky. The wet smell of scarred earth is all-pervasive.

As I stand here in the fold of a sliver of ancient temperate rainforest, a tan sessile oak leaf falls gently to the river bank. I reach out to grasp it, but a squally wind whips it away and hurls it into the narrow headwaters we call Sgithwen.

A leaf is not a leaf for ever. It is in a state of flux between leaf and particulates, living and dead. A leaf that falls in the stream is the beginning of a chain. Spin, yaw, pitch and submerge, it's hurried away downstream in a thrum of fluvial energy and I lose sight of it. The leaf has abruptly entered an ancient dynamic system of motion and unrest. Yesterday, Sgithwen was in full red-clay spate after downpours. Today, the water is clear and forceful. Tomorrow, who knows. The stream is different and yet the same. The water is also a blend of Sgithwen 'tea' percolated from surrounding organic and nonorganic matter, a mix of nutrients so unique that salmonids remember the smell, homing from the ocean to breed. The stream is different yet the same.

Heraclitus of Ephesus lived by the River Kayster in ancient Ionia. As I step into this stream, I hear his philosophy whispering down through two and half thousand years of algae-slippy boulders, 'Upon those who step into the same rivers different and different waters flow.' Heraclitus perceived, amongst nature's constant flux and opposites, an entity or one-ness. This something, the source of everything, he called 'Logos'. Life is an ever-changing continuum. Nothing remains the same, not least this stream in which I stand.

The river is a universal feature. Sgithwen stream falls to the River Wye, flowing to the River Severn and is channeled out to the ocean. But rivers are never exactly the same from one moment to another because their systems are constantly fluctuating. Evolving habitats downward along the gradient are described in science as a 'stream continuum'.

The fallen leaf up here in the hills is now food energy to be rationed downstream. As consumers in the food chain, freshwater insects called macro-invertebrates are great indicators of a healthy river ecosystem. They tend to follow this continuum in particular ways. Some, like the white-clawed crayfish, are keystone species and, being polytrophic, fill a multiplicity of roles in the river. Most are grouped to reflect their labours.

Shredders, such as freshwater shrimp and the smaller stonefly larvae, begin by tearing away at coarse organic material like our sessile oak leaf. Not all the leaf is consumed and much floats away downstream together with faeces, later to be consumed by collectors such as midge larvae, nematodes and worms. More particles are scavenged in and around the sediments. Further downstream, the widening reaches open up to sky and sun, encouraging the growth of periphyton, a mix of algae, bacteria and other microbes. *Grazers* such as mayfly larvae, cased caddis-fly larvae and river snails scrape it from submerged rocks and roots for sustenance.

Filterers like pearl mussels sift out still finer grains left in suspense, along with floating algae (including single-celled alga called diatoms), and nutrients washed from the flood plains. Invertebrate *predators*, such as dragonfly and large stonefly larvae, ambush other insects that have consumed our leaf. And in lower reaches and depths, the flow is laden with yet more life, in microscopic phytoplankton and zooplankton composed of dissolved carbon, the carbon that once embodied a veteran sessile oak. And so the unseen continue to be nurtured.

Autumn gives rise to this annual pulse of life in the river; in time, leaves help to form a bounty of other living beings, way beyond the water's edge. Predators move more easily up and down the continuum, feeding on in-stream and riparian life. There are pike, otters, the grey heron and, of course, humans, among others. Sand martins and Daubenton's bats hunt adult aquatic insects just as they emerge from the water.

One person's lifespan is a blink of an eye to the river, a leaf's existence even less so. My own perceptions of time may be faster than the sessile oak or the 100-year-old pearl mussel, slower than the caddisfly or fleet sand martin. Each species experiences the river uniquely. Ebb or flow, whirlpool or riffle, all senses engaged, memories in the making. The river is different yet the same.

Long into the future, perhaps the winds may turn, continents will divide again, and the river's entire length may disappear, devoured by geological action and climates. There may be traces of its ancient forms and life in the rock, and these may, in turn, erode to dust and silt the rivers a billion years from now. And so the story continues, beyond a simple lotic flow of water, of the autumnal leaf and the philosopher's river; the beginning of a chain, the nurturing of the unseen and a myriad of woven fabrics of life, of place and of time.

Ginny Battson, 2016

Is not this a true autumn day? Just the still melancholy that I love – that makes life and nature harmonise. The birds are consulting about their migrations, the trees are putting on the hectic or the pallid hues of decay, and begin to strew the ground, that one's very footsteps may not disturb the repose of earth and air, while they give us a scent that is a perfect anodyne to the restless spirit. Delicious autumn! My very soul is wedded to it, and if I were a bird I would fly about the earth seeking the successive autumns.

George Eliot, letter to Maria Lewis, Oct. 1, 1841

The Salvation Army brass band marched down St Michael's Road past Evans' chip shop, pom-pommed round the corner and up the little bit of hill to Elmsleigh Road and on down over the railway crossing to the seafront. The houses were very still and the streets empty but Mam's chatter ruffled the sabbath hush. Clennon Valley smelt of woodsmoke and tired trees. A flock of longtailed tits exploded from the hedgerow thorns and Mam and I crept along the brow of the sheep pasture gathering the mushrooms and dropping them into the basket. She wore old wellingtons and a green headscarf. The October sun lit the blond tresses stirring on her forehead; and to me she was the loveliest creature God had ever made. Golden brown countryside rolled around us. A buzzard skirled; a green woodpecker undulated away like a little kite being pulled behind a running child; rooks cawed from the stubble.

'That's pretty,' Mam said, and I followed her gaze.

Blue mist filled the lap of the valley and from it rose a heron, climbing through the sunshine and swinging west towards the Dart.

'I love autumn,' she continued.

Under the hedge a crow jauntily walked up the carcass of a sheep to get at the eyes.

'I like crows,' I said, knowing the remark would be unpopular.

'Crows peck out lambs' eyes, Bri.'

'Why did God make 'em then, Mam?'

'Maybe he don't care about animals. There's lots of things

he don't care about – like the little children who got killed when that German plane hit the church in Torquay.'

'I shot a bluetit with my catapult last Wednesday.'

'Why? Bluetits are lovely little birds.'

'I gave it to Tacker Willocks' ferret.'

'You mustn't kill songbirds, Bri. We used to feed our ferrets on sparrows in feather and chickens' heads. Never bluetits. Sparrows eat grain and there's lots of them.'

'Can I have an air pistol, Mam?'

'No you bloody can't. You're enough trouble as it is.'

'I'll run away from home.'

She grinned and said, 'Good.'

After the roast dinner which we ate around one o'clock Mam and Dad took me for a long walk. We went up Fisher Street, down Winner Street which was one of Paignton's oldest thoroughfares, climbed Colley End Road to Kings Ash and wandered out into the farmland. The lanes were deep, narrow and muddy. Buff- and brown-speckled oak leaves rustled down to swell the mush of yellow hazel and elm leaves in the red gruel. But we did not miss many of the filberts and at Blagdon Dad filled his pockets with walnuts.

The country road ran crookedly from Barton Pines to Totnes, passing high above the coombes and spinneys before dropping into the ancient hamlet of Berry Pomeroy. The vast panorama of South, West and Mid-Devon opened before us – a far-off glimpse of Dartmoor straight ahead and, to the left, hill upon rounded hill racing through the distant haze of the South Hams. One day I promised myself I'd walk to those dim horizons and discover what it was that saddened and excited me.

Sometimes Dad carried me on his shoulders whistling tunes like 'Roll out the Barrel' and 'Colonel Bogey', or singing snippets of gibberish:

'Articabs and choakajiz, ten barb roobi-a-stick' (Artichokes and cabbages, rhubarb ten bob a stick).

Then we headed for home up the main Totnes Road into dimpsey. From the hilltop we caught a glimpse of the sea and Berry Head lighthouse winking from the grey darkfall. And the churchbells rang out right across Devon, village and town taking up the music so that it filled every corner of Sunday.

Under the oxblood-coloured plough of Blagdon Hill the church of Collaton St Mary stood among tall trees, its windows glowing palely golden. Opposite the churchyard was a small meadow where the brook ran against the hedge. We stopped by the five-barred gate to feed the horses and Dad called to them, his voice thick with the affection that always flavoured his chats with animals. O the lovely Devon burr softening the Rs and the words turning on his tongue like earth behind the plough – heavy and rich.

The horses were suddenly there in the dimpsey, breathing the scent of crushed grass. Six dark shapes nuzzled each other and lifted their heads as if to drink the bell-music. Then they raced away to the shadows of the great, black elms. Those work animals found true liberty at dusk. They gazed from deep, mysterious dreams into fabled places where horses are kings. Turning to walk on I heard them thundering around the field and I heard them again yesterday when I re-read Dylan Thomas's 'Fern Hill'.

Brian Carter, Yesterday's Harvest, *1982*

The Wild Swans at Coole

The trees are in their autumn beauty,
The woodland paths are dry,
Under the October twilight the water
Mirrors a still sky;
Upon the brimming water among the stones
Are nine-and-fifty swans.

The nineteenth autumn has come upon me
Since I first made my count;
I saw, before I had well finished,
All suddenly mount
And scatter wheeling in great broken rings
Upon their clamorous wings.

I have looked upon those brilliant creatures,
And now my heart is sore.
All's changed since I, hearing at twilight,
The first time on this shore,
The bell-beat of their wings above my head,
Trod with a lighter tread.

Unwearied still, lover by lover,
They paddle in the cold
Companionable streams or climb the air;

Their hearts have not grown old;
Passion or conquest, wander where they will,
Attend upon them still.

But now they drift on the still water,
Mysterious, beautiful;
Among what rushes will they build,
By what lake's edge or pool
Delight men's eyes when I awake some day
To find they have flown away?

William Butler Yeats, 1917

I stand among the gnarled old apple trees and feel surrounded by a group of friends. The pruned shapes and the rough lichen-encrusted bark conjure up memories from my childhood in Kent, where orchards abounded and everyone had an apple tree or two in their garden. In my mind, I see clouds of pale pink flowers and rosy red fruits, set against a clear blue sky. I can feel the sun on my shoulders and smell the soft perfume of apples. This kaleidoscope of images is no respecter of order, for the seasons are muddled as they tumble over each other in my memory.

Today though, it is definitely autumn. There was a chill in the air this morning and dew drops were glistening on the cobwebs in the hedge. The leaves have turned a tired-looking green and some are distinctly yellow. This North Yorkshire orchard, planted by the local gentry in the nineteenth century, has had a varied life. Once tended, pruned and prized, it then fell out of favour and spent many years abandoned, ignored and unkempt. Now, it has a new lease of life with a gardener who is busy restoring these wonderful trees to their former glory. Each tree is an individual, tall and upright, wide and spreading or compact and stocky. There are many old varieties represented here with intriguing names like Bismarck, Keswick Codlin, Newton Wonder, Blenheim Orange and Peasgood's Nonsuch.

The rough grass and nettles under my feet have been scythed and the best of the crop harvested. The inaccessible fruits at the top of the trees and the rotten ones on the ground are all that are left. Perhaps originally pigs would have been driven in and left to feast on what they could find. But today we are going to collect the remaining fruit and convert it into apple juice. The beauty of making juice is that we can use scabby, misshapen and bruised fruit so that very little of the crop ever goes to waste.

We're making an early start and begin by selecting a tree, picking up the fallen apples and then spreading enormous sheets of plastic under it. We nudge the tree with apple pickers, long telescopic poles with a v-shaped fork on top. The fork holds a branch as we shake, encouraging a shower of apples, leaves, twigs, spiders and earwigs to cascade on to the sheets. On picking up the ends, the apples roll to the middle and we gather them into bags, jettisoning any that are too rotten. We move the plastic to the next tree and begin again.

Back at the farm we wash the apples. They don't have to be squeaky clean, but soil, mould and animal droppings must be removed or the juice will be contaminated. We then scrat them. This is a process that turns firm rounded apples into a sloppy pulp. Originally horse power and later steam would have been used to power two large wooden wheels with protruding fingers to rotate and interlock. The apples would have been dropped in and pulverised as they were squashed between the wheels. Today we are using an electric scratter which is like a garden shredder. This machine is very efficient but very noisy. It's a great sense of relief when it's switched off for a while and I become aware of the quiet world around me. I can now hear the distant squabbling rooks, the buzzing of insects and the chatter of my companions.

The apple pulp, or pomace, is a light yellow which quickly oxidises to a brown colour, in the same way that a discarded apple core would. The pulverising releases the characteristic apple perfume, which attracts dozens of wasps that hamper our progress. I realise the tangy smell is linked in my mind to the fear of these insects and their painful stings. I feel a bit edgy as I continue to work, trying to dodge these black and yellow terrors.

We're now ready to extract the apple juice and accomplish this by using a press. Today we're using a barrel press and a rack and cloth press, but the principle is the same for both. The pomace is placed in a cloth which is squeezed more and more tightly by a heavy weight. The cloth bag is held in a slatted barrel in the barrel press, and several bags are stacked up on wooden slats on the rack and cloth press.

The apple cores, skin and pips are retained by the cloth and the juice is able to flow freely through the pores so we can collect it in clean buckets.

Everyone wants to try the juice. I savour my cupful. It both looks and tastes like liquid gold. It is the best, purest apple juice I have ever drunk and when I close my eyes I can taste sunshine, fresh air and apple blossom. Each mouthful transports me, once again, to my orchard of gnarled old friends.

Janet Willoner, 2016

'Du's back then? Fine that. I hae something to tell dee . . . '
The old crofter pauses, weighing the awkwardness of what he has to say.

'Something's been takkin' dy hens. I doot it's da draatsi.'

The clocks went back the day before I returned home to Shetland. As I step outside into an unusually still, moonless October evening, I can hear the lisping calls of countless redwings as they stream overhead, invisible in the absolute darkness. The air is heavy with moisture, and below me the sea sloughs rhythmically on the shingle beach at the foot of my small croft. I open the metal gate that leads into the grassy yard where my hens live, and play my torch across the door of the old stone byre in which they roost at night. The pop-hole in the door is still open – night had fallen well before I got home.

There are neither streetlights nor immediate neighbouring houses here. My croft stands alone on the brow of a promontory at the north-eastern tip of one of Shetland's smaller inhabited islands. My neighbours are the grey seals that watch me curiously from the sea, and my visitors at this time of year are the migrant birds that have blown in from Scandinavia. The news that an otter has been taking my hens while I've been away seems unlikely – in the ten years I have lived here in the islands I have never had any bother with them. Their local reputation seems entirely out of proportion with the reality of the charismatic animals I have spent many hours tracking and watching on the island. Apparently it's not just domestic poultry that needs to worry about them:

'When da draatsi bites du, he'll no slip dee until he hears dy bones crack.'

This is all at odds with my time spent sharing their lives in their coastal territories. I have lain in the glistening, slimy bronze straps of kelp at low tide watching adolescent siblings twisting and turning in a Medusan knot as they play-fight mere yards from me. I have watched otters hunting slippery butter-fish, misshapen lumpsuckers and writhing octopuses, tracking their trail of exhaled bubbles on the water's surface as they dive again and again until a catch is made and they swim in to land to consume it. I have watched them noisily courting one another, have listened to the anxious whistling of cubs unseen in their holt, and have seen their mother drive them away when they've grown up and should be seeking territories of their own.

But I've never lost a hen to them.

Rough edges of stamped-down turves stop me in my tracks as I walk to the byre. There are muddy bootprints in the glistening wet grass and, sticking to them, myriad small, pathetic downy white feathers.

'I've buried aa dat wis left. I didna ken what tae do. I doot du widna want dem cast ower da banks.'

Poor Lawrie, left in charge of feeding the free-ranging hens, has been left to clear away the remains of a daily incursion that has lasted a fortnight. 'I ken dy peerie boy has names fur aa dem . . .'

Lawrie is right – my young son named all of the hens and I am dreading breaking the news to him. As I stand unhappily looking down at their rough grave, treacherously wishing Lawrie had chosen somewhere less obvious in which to bury them, I am suddenly struck by the most uncomfortable feeling that someone – *something* – is nearby.

I swing the torch to my left and there, just beyond the wire fence that bounds the field, are a pair of dull red glowing eyes. The eyeshine is almost at the top of the fence. This is deeply unnerving and my immediate thought, irrationally, is that a large dog is watching me silently from the darkness. My stomach clenches slightly in what, I am later ashamed to admit, is primal fear.

'Go on! Away with you! Go home!' I shout at it. The eyes don't move. 'Go on!'

I start walking towards them. The eyeshine suddenly drops, comes and goes quickly as the animal casts from side to side, and then vanishes altogether. In the weak light at the end of the torch's beam I see a large, long dark shape humping and slouching unhurriedly away down the track to the road. It's an otter, and a big one at that. Where he stood upright I find a perfect round hole worn through the long thick grass at the base of the fence. This is where he's been coming and going. The gaps in the wire are too small to pull a hen through, but are just big enough to allow the passage of a determined male otter. I will later learn that this is where Lawrie found a dead hen every morning, partially consumed as far from the byre as the otter could remove it.

In the mud around the byre door are footprints. Those of the hens, and the distinctive pugmarks of an otter. My impression of size is borne out now – this is as big an otter as I've ever seen. The paw prints come and go, some fresh and some older and more obscure. Having found a ready food source he's been returning to exploit it. The naturalist in me dispassionately notes this; the crofter and the father in me is upset, dismayed that our blameless and tame hens have been decimated.

I shut the pop-hole in the byre door. If I feel angry, it is at myself. Mostly I feel guilty – perhaps I should have left the hens shut indoors while I was away? Has ten years of their free-ranging without consequence allowed me to grow complacent? I walk back to the house contemplating a weekend of building a small, heavily wired outside run for the hens.

Coming home on Friday evening I see a familiar and tragic sight by the roadside. Where the narrow road bisects my croft, an otter has been hit by a car. An all too common sight in Shetland, where otters exist in such high numbers but have never learned to associate danger with moving vehicles. I stoop to examine it. There is no helping this unfortunate animal – it is freshly dead, the body still warm, a small pool of vivid blood on the asphalt beneath its muzzle. This is my otter – a large, heavy old male, his size imposing even in death. His nose is badly scarred, his eyes rheumy and his claws worn and blunt. Prising open his jaws I find he is missing most of his teeth, and those that remain are in poor condition.

After a life of roaming and fathering cubs around Whalsay he will have been finding catching fish an increasingly difficult task as age caught up with him and his physical condition deteriorated. At this time of year, with daylight hours rapidly dwindling and the weather deteriorating, his ability to hunt successfully will have been further impaired. Having chanced upon my hens he would have been unable to resist such easy pickings. Under the cover of darkness he had been returning from the shore to the byre to see if the pop-hole was open again. He was well into the autumn of his life, but now it has prematurely come to an end.

I pick him up, and carry him to the house. Tomorrow I won't be building anything. I will be burying an otter next to the remains of his last supper.

Jon Dunn, 2016

October

The green elm with the one great bough of gold
Lets leaves into the grass slip, one by one, –
The short hill grass, the mushrooms small milk-white,
Harebell and scabious and tormentil,
That blackberry and gorse, in dew and sun,
Bow down to; and the wind travels too light
To shake the fallen birch leaves from the fern;
The gossamers wander at their own will.
At heavier steps than birds' the squirrels scold.

The rich scene has grown fresh again and new
As Spring and to the touch is not more cool
Than it is warm to the gaze; and now I might
As happy be as earth is beautiful,
Were I some other or with earth could turn
In alternation of violet and rose,
Harebell and snowdrop, at their season due,
And gorse that has no time not to be gay.
But if this be not happiness, – who knows?
Some day I shall think this a happy day,
And this mood by the name of melancholy
Shall no more blackened and obscured be.

Edward Thomas, 1917

*B*y the bus stop, near the bridge, at the back of the industrial estate, along the garden fence . . . the seasonal memo is everywhere. Friends get called. While juveniles reclaim last year's hexagonal jam jars from neighbours, adults rustle up boots, bags, and boxes. Because when starlings murmur, conkers fall, geese flock, deer rut, trees blush and fungi emerge . . . humans go blackberrying.

For the bramble, it's already been a busy morning. It has been sung from by a robin, whiskered by an acrobating mouse and plundered by a mistle thrush who, knocking ripe berries to the ground, activated a sweet-toothed vole. And now it has an appointment with another forager; except that this one, from the sound of it, is travelling in a herd.

Leaving the main path, we head down a tiny track, catching up about bike rides, beaches and BBQs and who hasn't got round to sorting out school uniforms. Our cubs, scurrying ahead, yelp with anticipation. They're old enough now to know the way, because they came here last year, and the year before, and the year before that, and their internal map is bright with indelible landmarks. Here you fell in the mud. There we met the fox. By the stream, we sat in the lap of that massive oak, mum, mum, mum, mum, remember?

The bramble isn't in favour of large mammals as they have a habit of eating young plants. Birds are preferable, a point the bramble makes clear by spacing out its thorns so that small feathery guests have easy access, and big hairy gate-crashers don't. Compared to birds and small mammals, larger ones, with their slow moving stand-and-eat habits, are useless at – to put it delicately – 'distribution'.

Someone tells a story about his grandmother and her ancient hooked stick. She kept it in the shed and only ever got it out to go blackberrying. Oh, how they loved the ritual! How she, stiff-hipped, would part the brambles with the stick and send him further into the thicket to collect the fruit she could no longer reach. How she would rinse the berries in the tin bath, while he designed this year's labels.

A gut's a gut, whoever it belongs to, but the bramble hands out its flavour-favours judiciously, dangling its bribes in a drip-drip of staggered ripening. Keep 'em hungry, keep 'em keen. An over-fed bird is, after all, a useless messenger, when it comes to spreading the bramble gospel. The remnants of the blossom still cling like down around the base of a small, green berry, a hard knobbly dome. You can hardly call it a blackberry at all; more like an after-flower; a fruit-to-be; a *bramble-idea*. Next to it hang other berries in various hues: clumps of mottled pink, scarlet, burgundy. Their colour is their cunning. Not this, it means. Not me. Not yet. Seek elsewhere.

Murmur and wow. All around, brambles sparkle with baubles. Our pack spreads out in an optimal foraging pattern, obeying the bramble's code. Eyes register (but don't see) the greens, hands brush past the reds and reach as commanded for the plumpest, blackest, juiciest treasure. Let the picking begin!

The bramble has already got the job started. While its green and red berries remain bound tight to its stems, the bramble has obligingly loosened the ripe ones. It *throws* fruit!

Sometimes we fumble the catch and the blackberries fall. Mostly, though, it takes just a gentle flick of the finger to beckon the berries into palms. Look, that one, and the next one, and those over there, the seduction of the prizes stronger than the punishment of the thorns. Tiptoeing and turning, we dance to the tune of the bramble. Silence falls, along with breathing and pulse rates. Never mind antioxidants, vitamins and fibre; here is health, and the eating hasn't even started (except for one of our young, tucked in a sunny corner, berry-ink on her lips). Time slows down, speeds up. Bramble Zen.

The bramble draws blood. But its crop is decimated: we apes have been thorough. Tomorrow's birds will have to fly further for their breakfast. The small mammals' tummies will rumble, and the badger, hedgehog and fox won't linger here tonight.

Tamsin Constable, 2016

Gossamer, as it is called, being the fine web of certain species of spiders, floating in the air in abundance, and lodging on the trees, or the rigging of ships, and on other objects, affords a sign of fine settled weather in autumn, as does the much covering of the ground and herbage by the woof of the spiders in general.

In crossing the Channel from Calais to Dover, I have observed that the captains of the vessels have sometimes forboded fine settled weather from the settling on the masts and rigging, of certain sort of web, which we take to be the woof of some spider, though we have observed it to alight on the ships when some way out at sea.

Thomas Furly Forster, The Pocket Encyclopaedia of Natural Phenomena, *published 1827*

As a child I often dreamed of living in a treehouse built in the branches of an ancient oak. I would press my ear against the oak tree, willing to hear its message to me, certain, as children often are, that there was a message to be heard. As I've grown, the most magical thing about the woodland has become the thing that you have to focus a little more closely to notice: the creation of the trees I so love.

For grey squirrels and woodland birds, autumn is a busy season: a time for fattening up and preparing for the coming quiet; and for creating stores that will allow them to survive when food is scarce. Acorns, and other nuts and seeds, are a vital food source for these creatures. And that's how a simple, yet special relationship has developed between them and the trees in their woodland habitat.

A common sight is a squirrel, ignorant to all else, busying itself with burying acorns in seemingly random spots, ready to unearth later. Sit patiently at the foot of a tree, and you will be rewarded by the glimpse of a fluffy tail as the squirrel scampers down to search for bounty.

Intent on the task at hand, it rummages through piles of golden leaves until it finds what it's looking for. After an inspection, the acorn is carried away to what has been deemed a suitable place, and in less than a minute it's efficiently buried. And then the process starts over again, countless times. It can quickly become hypnotic if you sit and watch.

But it isn't random, this process. The squirrel isn't simply

114

choosing an acorn and burying it. It is systematically examining and scrutinising its prize. It's evaluating the benefit of burying each nut, deciding whether to store it for later or enjoy it now. High value nuts, those that will provide more nutrition and are less likely to perish, are the most likely to be buried as they will survive longer, ensuring much needed provisions for this and other squirrels to unearth in the coming winter.

Due to their excellent memory and sense of smell, squirrels track down much of their hoard later on. However, there are inevitably caches that get missed. And that is the simple beauty of the system. Squirrels, and other distributors such as jays, are vital to trees because, in order to successfully take root and thrive, the seeds or nuts need to be distributed farther from their parent tree than is possible for them to fall. If they take root too close, they will be blocked from the sun by their parent's foliage. Not only that, those high value nuts, the ones specifically chosen to be buried, are more likely to set root, because of their quality.

That first act of burying a treat is the first step towards the life of a new tree. There's an almost beautiful art to this. A symbiotic relationship that ensures both tree and squirrel survive to the next generation. At first glance, autumn appears to be the season of harvest, signalling the end of that year's new life. But when you look more closely you can see it's actually the opposite. It's the beginning of a new cycle. Let's imagine in the next hundred years those tiny acorns standing proud and strong in their woodland, with a little girl pressing her ear to them, hoping to hear a secret.

Leanne Manchester, 2016

Oh God. What am I doing here? I'm sitting on a white plastic picnic chair under the shade of a marquee roof. Ten feet behind me Mabel resembles a shadow cast on water; her wings are crossed as tight as swords and her eyes bloom huge with horror. I know how she feels. *Too many people,* I think, fidgeting on my seat. *Too many people.*

'So, Helen,' Stuart had said. 'The landowner's asked us to bring some hawks along for Apple Day at the farm.'

'Apple Day?'

Stuart told me that it was a tiny country fair, a celebration of rural history, farming and local food. 'We're not flying, just weathering the hawks in a marquee so members of the public can see them. I'll take my tiercel. Greg's bringing his barbary. Alan's coming up with some eagles. Can you bring Mabel?'

'Yes, of course,' I said. 'No problem.' I could do this. I'd worked in a falconry centre, for God's sake. All I did for months was show people hawks. But as the day grew closer I started to fret. *How will Mabel cope?* Two months ago she was a bomb-proof, crowd-proof goshawk. But goshawks aren't like other hawks: they need constant carriage to stay tame. Now we're living in the empty suburbs we've not seen people for weeks. She's forgotten how not to be scared of people. *And so have I.* My teeth are clenched so tight in the face of the crowds I feel pain blossoming up my jaw.

After twenty minutes Mabel raises one foot. It looks ridiculous. She is not relaxed enough to fluff out her feathers; she still resembles a wet and particoloured seal. But she makes this small concession to calmness, and she stands there like a man with one hand resting on the gearstick. She looks pathetically small next to the birds beside her. To her left is a golden eagle, a hulking great thing with chest-feathers like armoured scales and taloned feet the size of human hands. To her right is a male martial eagle, an antelope-killing black and white monster with piercing white eyes. It is enormous, bigger than most of the dogs walking past the mesh fence in front of the marquee, and it watches them go by with its black chrysanthemum-petalled crest raised in idle speculation of murder.

Stuart has brought his tiercel peregrine. Greg has brought his barbary falcon, a tiny jewelled dusty-blue and copper falcon with thin golden toes. While it preens he sits cross-legged, chatting with members of the public, his red cashmere jumper holed wildly at the elbow. Alan the eagle-man is drinking tea from a plastic cup, resting an arm on the tall perch of a saker falcon, which looks up at him with a mild and playful eye.

I can't sit still. I go for a walk round the fair. It is not very big, but it is full of surprising things. Smoke from an oil-drum barbecue curling through drying chestnut leaves. Beneath the tree an ancient wooden cider press pouring apple juice into cups. The crushed apples fall into mounds of oxidising pulp beside it and the man working the mechanism is shouting something to the craggy plantsman on the next stand with stripling trees for sale. I find a cake stand, a face-painting stand, a stand of vivaria full of snakes, spiders and stick insects the size of your hand. A stall of orange pumpkins by an ice-cream van. A boy kneeling by a hutch staring at a rabbit under a paper sign that says MY NAME IS FLOPSEY. 'Hello, Flopsey,' he says, bringing his hand up to the wire. I walk into a white marquee, and inside, in dim green shade, find trestle-tables displaying hundreds of apple varieties. Some are the size of a hen's egg; some are giant, sprawling cookers you'd need two hands to hold. Each variety sits in a labelled wooden compartment. I walk slowly among the apples, glorying in their little differences. Soft orange, streaked with tiger-spots of pink. *Charles Ross. Berkshire pre 1890. Dual use.* A little one with bark-like blush markings over a pale green ground. *Coronation. Sussex 1902. Dessert.* Miniature green boulders, the side in shadow deep rose. *Chivers Delight. Cambridgeshire 1920. Dessert.* Huge apple, deep yellow with hyperspace-spotting of rich red. *Peasgood's Nonsuch. Lincolnshire 1853. Dual use.*

The apples cheer me. The stalls have too. I decide the fair is a wonderful thing. I wander back to my chair, and as Mabel relaxes, so do I. I wolf down a burger, gossip with my falconer friends. Stories are told, jokes are made, old grievances aired, the qualities and abilities and flights of various hawks discussed in minute detail. It strikes me suddenly how much British falconry has changed since the days of Blaine and White. Back then it was the secretive, aristocratic sport of officers and gentlemen. In Germany, falconry had fed into the terrible dreams of an invented Ayran past. Yet here we are now in all our variousness. A carpenter ex-biker, a zookeeper ex-soldier, two other zookeepers, an electrician and an erstwhile historian. Four men, two women, two eagles, three falcons and a goshawk. I swig from a bottle of cider and this company is suddenly all I'd ever wished for.

Helen Macdonald, H is for Hawk, 2014

Evidence (Long-eared Owls)

Each winter, they shrink to a rumour.
For years, only a low moan
that might have been wind blowing
across the chimney pots,
or a creak and whine
that could have been the rusting gate,
swinging wide just this side of sleep.

But once, half a mile from home
and surprised by the silent swoop
of night, we flushed a flurry
of autumn colour in the lane
and were almost brushed by a breath
of wings, that hardened and darkened
amid the hawthorn thicket, became
a branch tipped by embers

burning up the light's last slivers.
Freed from earth's embrace, with every star
a crucible to kindle from,
so might our eyes fire.
So might we flame on.

Matt Merritt, 2011

A rich tint of russet deepened on the forest top, and seemed to sink day by day deeper into the foliage like a stain; riper and riper it grew, as an apple colours. Broad acres these of the last crop, the crop of leaves; a thousand thousand quarters, the broad earth will be their barn. A warm red lies on the hill-side above the woods, as if the red dawn stayed there through the day; it is the heath and heather seeds; and higher still, a pale yellow fills the larches. The whole of the great hill glows with colour under the short hours of the October sun; and overhead, where the pine-cones hang, the sky is of the deepest azure. The conflagration of the woods burning luminously crowds into those short hours a brilliance the slow summer does not know.

The frosts and mists and battering rains that follow in quick succession after the equinox, the chill winds that creep about the fields, have ceased a little while, and there is a pleasant sound in the fir trees. Everything is not gone yet. In the lanes that lead down to the 'shaws' in the dells, the 'gills', as these wooded depths are called, buckler ferns, green, fresh, and elegantly fashioned, remain under the shelter of the hazel-lined banks. From the tops of the ash wands, where the linnets so lately sang, coming up from the stubble, the darkened leaves have been blown, and their much-divided branches stand bare like outstretched fingers. Black-spotted sycamore leaves are down, but the moss grows thick and deeply green; and the trumpets of the lichen seem to be larger, now they are moist, than when they were dry under the summer heat. Here is herb Robert in flower – its leaves are scarlet; a leaf of St. John's-wort, too, has become scarlet; the bramble leaves are many shades of crimson; one plant of tormentil has turned yellow. Furze bushes, grown taller since the spring, bear a second bloom, but not perhaps so golden as the first. It is the true furze, and not the lesser gorse; it is covered with half-opened buds; and it is clear, if the short hours of sun would but lengthen, the whole gorse hedge would become aglow again. Our trees, too, that roll up their buds so tightly, like a dragoon's cloak, would open them again at Christmas; and the sticky horse-chestnut would send forth its long ears of leaves for New Year's Day. They would all come out in leaf again if we had but a little more sun; they are quite ready for a second summer.

Brown lie the acorns, yellow where they were fixed in their cups; two of these cups seem almost as large as the great acorns from abroad. A red dead-nettle, a mauve thistle, white and pink bramble flowers, a white strawberry, a little yellow tormentil, a broad yellow dandelion, narrow hawkweeds, and blue scabious, are all in flower in the lane. Others are scattered on the mounds and in the meads adjoining, where may be collected some heath still in bloom, prunella, hypericum, white yarrow, some heads of red clover, some beautiful buttercups, three bits of blue veronica, wild chamomile, tall yellowwood, pink centaury, succory, dock cress, daisies, fleabane, knapweed, and delicate blue harebells. Two York roses flower on the hedge: altogether, twenty-six flowers, a large bouquet for October 19, gathered, too, in a hilly country.

Besides these, note the broad hedge-parsley leaves, tunnelled by leaf-miners; bright masses of haws gleaming in the sun; scarlet hips; great brown cones fallen from the spruce firs; black heart-shaped bindweed leaves here, and buff bryony leaves yonder; green and scarlet berries of white bryony hanging thickly on bines from which the leaves have withered; and bunches of grass, half yellow and half green, along the mound. Now that the leaves have been brushed from the beech saplings you may see how the leading stem rises in a curious wavy line; some of the leaves lie at the foot, washed in white dew, that stays in the shade all day; the wetness of the dew makes the brownish red of the leaf show clear and bright. One leaf falls in the stillness of the air slowly, as if let down by a cord of gossamer gently, and not as a stone falls – fate delayed to the last. A moth adheres to a bough, his wings half open, like a short brown cloak flung over his shoulders. Pointed leaves, some drooping, some horizontal, some fluttering slightly, still stay on the tall willow wands, like bannerets on the knights' lances, much torn in the late battle of the winds. There is a shower from a clear sky under the trees in the forest; brown acorns rattling as they fall, and rich coloured Spanish chestnuts thumping the sward, and sometimes striking you as you pass under; they lie on the ground in pocketfuls. Specks of brilliant scarlet dot the grass like some bright berries blown from the bushes; but on stooping to pick them, they are found to be the heads of a fungus. Near by lies a black magpie's feather, spotted with round dots of white.

Richard Jefferies, 'Just before Winter' from Field and Hedgerow:
The Last Essays of Richard Jefferies, *1889*

Watchers in the Woods

Under trees, mushroom-moist air lingered,
Movement in the murk revealed two watchers:
Roe deer lifted heads and skittered in gloom.

In stretching shadows, we held our spots, slowed
Our breaths. Watching, deciding our next moves.
Fawn moved to mother – comfort, connection

Both so delicate, I paused, sure a shift
Would send them tripping in decaying scrub
Snapping graceful slender thoroughbred legs.

Birds called again and still we stood, heads up.
Russet-smooth coats, leaf-dappled, ears fine-tuned.
They took a step on ballerina toes,
At first stiff-legged, then grazing as they went.
We travelled the woods on parallel paths.

Brush barred us from full view, letting them keep
Their offended-cat pretence of not spotting me,
Until they passed from sight.

Had they watched, deciding to ask me in,
As I was finally leaving?

Julia Wallis, 2016

'It's alive!' announced the older boy.

Mum, ruddy-cheeked, lips pursed in concentration, looked into the pan of limp, grey lifeless worm-like creatures in simmering milk; stared at the elver on the kitchen floor, turned back to the pan on the stove and gave its fishy mixture a stir.

'I said it wasn't dead.'

My brother carefully scooped up this remarkable creature, slipped it into an empty coffee jar he fished out from underneath the sink and filled it with water straight from the tap.

Such was my first encounter with the European eel (*Anguilla anguilla*). Many species exhibit incredible survival tendencies, but the eel's pertinacity – whether the European, American, African, Asian or Australasian member of the family *Anguillidae*, is a wonder of the natural world.

Elvers once caught off the western shores of Europe in their hundreds of millions were sold at Gloucester fishmongers in 1970 for as little as ten pence per pound. They had already crossed several thousand miles of Atlantic Ocean from their nursery grounds of the Sargasso Sea in the Gulf of Mexico. Drifting through the North Atlantic's Gulf Stream for a year, maybe three, each larva undergoes a gradual metamorphosis from a tiny oval leaf shape into a transparent miniature version of its parents.

Glass eels begin to appear in estuaries of Europe and North Africa from December onwards, but in Britain are most strongly associated with extreme high tides of the spring equinox and

Easter; synonymous with tidal bores of the Bristol Channel, that push the translucent tiny eels (as they darken they are called 'elvers') further into freshwater. From large, muddy lowland rivers to rivulet mountain streams, the eel rarely considers anything off-limits: rocky waterfalls dripping with mosses and liverworts, shallow pools, abandoned mill-leats, farm ponds, isolated reservoirs, lakes stocked with hefty carp, ditches seemingly devoid of life or large canals used by container ships from the Far East are all sought out.

I know this because these are the places I went to find them, to catch them; the waterways and water-bodies of western Britain. Wherever I went, I searched; whatever the occasion, they were never far from my thoughts. Eels played with my imagination. I thought of their haunts and longevity; their diet and how to catch them.

Eels didn't feel like an obsession at the time, but they must have been, especially when my friends banned me from talking about them. At nineteen I moved to Wales and eels fell off my radar, along with the people who teased me about this fishy preoccupation.

Except every October, when diminishing daylight coincides with one final blast of heat, giving rise to a nearly sultry night. Nights when eels slide out from under sunken logs and boulders, underwater lairs that might have been home for a few years, or perhaps decades. Time enough for the yellow belly of its post-elver life to transform into a shiny, silvery ventral colour, the hallmark of an adult eel as it prepares itself for an out-migration to the sea.

Intrinsically linked to the seasons, the pattern of movements of eels seems unaltered for millennia, but all has not been well with *A. anguilla*. A collapse in catches of glass eels in the 1990s pointed to a catastrophic decline in populations of the species throughout its natural range. They became like eel gold, with elvers of the European eel fetching prices of £1,000 per kilogram in the fish markets of Tokyo and Beijing. On rivers in the West Country there was a frisson of tension as more and more fishermen used their traditional boat-shaped dip nets to scoop out the fewer and fewer eel larvae that rounded the muddy promontories of rivers Parrett, Usk, Wye and Severn.

Elver fishing drew attention to the eel's plight, but the increasing multitude of obstacles posed by the modern world are perhaps the greatest reason for its fall. A polluted world where adult eels are found with highly elevated levels of the insecticide dieldrin in their body tissues, where a parasite of the swim bladder – *Anguillicoloides crassus* – endemic in the Japanese eel, wormed its way into the wild European population. Combined with massive losses of wetland habitat, canalisation of once wild rivers and streams, concrete weirs, pumping houses and cooling water intakes at power stations where enormous numbers of eels perished, it seemed as if humans had cooked up a cocktail of recrimination against this ancient species.

Counter-intuitively perhaps, it was the loss of adult silver eels rather than their Sargasso offspring that gave greatest cause for concern. At Llangorse Lake (Llyn Syfaddon) in the Brecon Beacons National Park there had been immense numbers of silver eel caught at the eel-trap and sent to be smoked and sold to upmarket restaurants in the 1980s and 1990s.

Llangorse Lake, a place of mythical aquatic beasts and monster pike, is the largest natural lake in southern Wales and nestles under peculiarly shaped mountains and a landscape that harks back to a wilder, medieval time; turning up time and again in Welsh folk tales of slain heroes and villains and drowned prehistoric citadels. It is also a place for eels.

Documentary evidence has been found of eels being trapped here as long ago as 1584, which probably means they have been hunted and caught in the same two or three weeks at the end of October into November for many hundreds, if not thousands of years – a date in the seasonal calendar that existed long before our current concept of calendars.

What was it that made Llangorse such an attractive place for those in pursuit of eel? The answer lies along the tiny stream, the Afon Llynfi, a small river which flows from the lake until it meets the River Wye at Hay-on-Wye. It is the only way in and the only way out for a migratory eel (unless elvers are put into the lake, as has happened in recent times). Silver eels would have had to run the gauntlet of the small, narrow stream when our ancestors would have competed with bittern, otter and other fish-eating predators that would have congregated to reap some of this autumnal harvest leaving the great lake.

The trap came later and must have been devastatingly effective as it blocked the way of all the silver eels heading out under a full moon in late October. In just a couple of weeks in October 1989, over 2,500 lbs of eel were caught by operating the sluices of the trap. By the late 1990s the numbers were down to a fraction of that and the trap fell into disrepair.

However, it is now possible to use the trap to monitor how many of these juveniles reach adulthood and pass through it in the direction of the sea each autumn. We will never know the exact number that make it back to the Gulf of Mexico but the data collected at Llangorse could provide timely information to help introduce conservation measures for a species that has been declared as endangered as the giant panda.

My own odyssey with the eel began with a slippery elver that leapt out of a saucepan of milk; I have sometimes wondered what happened to that survivor that my brother helped into a coffee jar.

He kept it for several years in much the same way as you might have kept a goldfish won at a travelling fair; feeding it occasionally and leaving it bored and stunted in a windowsill in the dining room until, perhaps under instruction from a higher authority to tidy things up, or maybe through tedium, he took it down to the local river one afternoon and we watched it disappear into the silty bottom. It may not have lasted a day, but I like to imagine that it continued to survive and started to grow until it went from gold into silver and set off downstream to the sea one balmy late October evening.

Julian Jones, 2016

Bats flitting about late in the evening in spring and autumn, at which seasons they are most commonly seen, foretell fine day on the morrow, as do dorbeetles, and some other insects.

Thomas Furly Forster, The Pocket Encyclopaedia
of Natural Phenomena, *published 1827*

For most naturalists, autumn is a time to gently slow down; to rest, reflect and prepare for winter; to embrace a sense of mellow fruitfulness, by easing into life in the slow lane. Not in my experience. Hardcore birders see it differently. For us, autumn is the time to ramp it up. As the weather intensifies and Atlantic depressions batter the country, so birding ambitions heighten. Our willingness to travel vast distances increases, driven by a determination to see lost or migrant birds that seek shelter and sustenance on our shores.

Everything seems possible for the birder at this time of year. Nature, in all its mystery and diversity, can be neatly categorised, reduced down to a tick on a list. Speed of reaction and planning is key. Watch the weather charts mid-week like a hawk. Fill the car with petrol Friday evening, ready to rush to Aberdeen in time for dawn on a Saturday and on to Felixstowe by Sunday, all the while glorying in the deeply unsustainable and collectively selfish behaviour serviced by our burning need to connect with birds.

All across Britain's wild Atlantic edge, birders converge on lonely islands set in churning seas, on clustered archipelagos and notable promontories, be they spits, points or headlands. These places are indelibly carved into the psyche of the modern British birder. The birding geography and topography of autumnal Britain is a mix of venerable tradition, pioneering discovery, eternal hope – and catastrophic folly if you are trapped in the wrong place, personal agony setting in, knowing the rarities are elsewhere. These coastal landforms speak to us of past triumphs, drives through the night with expectations riding high, of camaraderie and a shared fellowship as another bird tumbles onto a cherished life list.

We gather but twice a year, this national ornithological tribe: first, rather tamely at the thronged British Birdwatching Fair in August at Rutland Water, mainly to swap stories and buy paraphernalia; again in the autumn, in a more disparate, loose but more purposeful way, smaller gangs out a-hunting rarities from Shetland to Scilly, captivated by the spectacle of migration.

The Isles of Scilly still offer a magical autumn birding season, where east meets west in a heady mix of species vagrancy from the USA to Siberia, attracting 450 or so birders from late September through to early November each year. That crowd is small compared with the invading army we once were back in the mid-1980s (1,500 visiting birders on islands with a resident population of just 2,200). By the hallowed month of October 1999, remembered fondly as almost birding perfection, numbers were down to 900.

We're still there, extending the tourism season by an extra month, bringing welcome income and endless bird news chatter from island to island on our handheld radios, but we no longer carry as much economic clout. For a host of reasons ranging from Scilly-fatigue, cost of travel and accommodation, prevailing weather systems, a slavish nervous fixation with the autumnal position of the jet stream, information technology and cheaper foreign birding trips, the meteoric rise of Shetland (yes, all of it, not just mythical Fair Isle!) over the past decade has put nails in the coffin of the much-loved Scilly season. Now, more than 500 visiting birders spread themselves thinly across that northern Viking landscape, bringing ornithological expertise, a crusading spirit and the tourist pound. Shetland lacks the intimacy and warmth of Scilly, but it offers exciting frontier birding in places. Birdforum (our gossip hub with over 147,000 members and 3.3 million posts) now runs an annual autumn Scilly-versus-Shetland competition for birders online in which each rare bird is ascribed a 'rarity value' based on previous occurrences. The battle lines are drawn in late September. Competition is fierce, often scornful or resentful.

Meanwhile, out east, the North Sea-fronting coastline of Britain from the Northern Isles to Dungeness is littered at weekends with folk kicking *Suaeda* bushes along Blakeney Point; thrashing about in dunes at Spurn; assiduously working stone walls on Fair Isle; extricating waifs from Heligoland traps; or gazing longingly into Shetland geos looking for a brief flash of movement to bring cheer to an overcast autumn day – perhaps even bestow some degree of ornithological immortality on the finder.

For an entire season your personal geographical and social (or anti-social) life is governed by the vibrations and beeps of a Rare Bird Alert (RBA) pager attached to your belt like some sort of life-affirming pacemaker. At times it even seems to be in tune with the beating of your heart. RBA send out nearly 110,000 messages annually to subscribers about scarce and rare birds. Some days in the autumn, if the weather is right for epic falls of migrants, 750 messages are sent out: a dizzying one message every minute and a half. That's frantic. The keyboard is on fire. The pager has a 'mega' override programmed in so that I can be summoned insistently at all times of the day. It urges me to drop everything, to get in the car and go. It once went off at a conference in September. I delivered my paper, at speed, and dashed off, at greater speed, to Flamborough Head. I missed the lunch, but I did see the brown shrike.

Autumn can make or break the birder. Reputations are won and lost, often in a serendipitous instance. It can be stressful in the extreme. This is raw, exhausting, elemental, and grim at times. It is riddled with jealousy, intrigue and competitiveness. Hard-won local patches close to the sea are defended like a fortress. Sharing at times seems unthinkable. Autumn is also a brutal time for lost young birds driven onwards by their inbuilt migratory instinct. If that misfires, they may end up in the drink.

I used to think that there was a certain rhythm to all this, but there isn't. Autumn is the most unpredictable and tumultuous of times, for birders and the birds; truly life in the fast lane. It is all order and chaos. But then, so is nature.

Dr Rob Lambert, 2016

To one who loves the hills at every season, the blossoming is not the best of the heather. The best of it is simply its being there – is the feel of it under the feet. To feel heather under the feet after long abstinence is one of the dearest joys I know.

Scent – fragrance, perfume – is very much pertinent to the theme of life, for it is largely a by-product of the process of living. It may also be a by-product of fire, but then fire feeds on what lives or what has lived. Or of chemical action, but if there are obscure chemical processes at work in the dead stuff of the mountain, they give little indication to my nose. The smells I smell are of life, plant and animal. Even the good smell of earth, one of the best smells in the world, is a smell of life, because it is the activity of bacteria in it that sets up this smell.

Plants then, as they go through the business of living, emit odours. Some, like the honey scents of flowers, are an added allurement to the insects; and if, as with heather, the scent is poured out most recklessly in the heat of the sun, that is because it is then that the insects are out in strength. But in other cases – as the fir trees – the fragrance is the sap, is the very life itself. When the aromatic savour of the pine goes searching into the deepest recesses of my lungs, I know it is life that is entering. I draw life in through the delicate hairs of my nostrils. Pines, like heather, yield their fragrance to the sun's heat. Or when the foresters come, and they are cut, then their scent is strong. Of all the kinds that grow on the low reaches of these mountains, spruce throws the strongest perfume on the air when the saw goes through it. In hot sun it is almost like a ferment – like strawberry jam on the boil, but with a tang that tautens the membranes of nose and throat.

Of plants that carry their fragrance in their leaves, bog myrtle is the mountain exampler. This grey-green shrub fills the boggy hollows, neighboured by cotton-grass and sundew, bog asphodel and the spotted orchis, and the minute scarlet cups of the lichens. Its fragrance is cool and clean, and like the wild thyme it gives it most strongly when crushed.

The other shrub, juniper, is secretive with its scent. It has an odd habit of dying in patches, and when a dead branch is snapped, a spicy odour comes from it. I have carried a piece of juniper wood for months, breaking it afresh now and then to renew the spice. This dead wood has a grey silk skin, impervious to rain. In the wettest season, when every fir branch in the woods is sodden, the juniper is crackling dry and burns with a clear heat. There's nothing better under the girdle when scones are baking – unless perhaps small larch twigs, fed into a fire already banked. Once, striking thick loose snow from low juniper bushes before walking through them, I surprised myself by striking from them also a delectable fragrance, that floated on the wintry air.

Birch, the other tree that grows on the lower mountain slopes, needs rain to release its odour. It is a scent with body to it, fruity like old brandy, and on a wet warm day, one can be as good as drunk with it. Acting through the sensory nerves, it confuses the higher centres; one is excited, with no cause that the wit can define.

Birch trees are least beautiful when fully clothed. Exquisite when the opening leaves just fleck them with points of green flame, or the thinning leaves turn them to a golden lace, they are loveliest of all when naked. In a low sun, the spun silk floss of their twigs seems to be created out of light. Without transfiguration, they are seen to be purple – when the sap is rising, a purple so glowing that I have caught sight of a birchwood on a hillside and for one incredulous moment thought the heather was in bloom.

Among drifts of these purple glowing birches, an occasional rowan looks dead; its naked boughs are a smooth white-grey, almost ghastly as the winter light runs over them. The rowan's moment is in October, when even the warmth of its clustering berries is surpassed by the blood-red brilliance of its leaves. This is the 'blessed quicken wood', that has power against the spirits of evil. It grows here and there among birches and firs, as a rule singly, and sometimes higher than either, a solitary bush by the rivulet in a ravine.

October is the coloured month here, far more brilliant than June, blazing more sharply than August. From the gold of the birches and bracken on the low slopes, the colour spurts upwards through all the creeping and inconspicuous growths that live among the heather roots – mosses that are lush green, or oak-brown, or scarlet, and the berried plants, blaeberry, cranberry, crowberry and the rest. Blaeberry leaves are a flaming crimson, and they are loveliest of all in the Rothiemurchus Forest, where the fir trees were felled in the 1914 War, and round and out of each stump blaeberry grows in upright sprigs: so that in October a multitude of pointed flames seem to burn upwards all over the moor.

Nan Shepherd, The Living Mountain: A Celebration
of the Cairngorm Mountains in Scotland, *1977*

Two hours of sailing off the glorious Isles of Scilly in October had landed us with a fair few gulls, a random juvenile puffin, some guillemots and four harbour porpoises. As the autumn plodded on, the chances of encountering huge rafts of seabirds had greatly diminished; a few weeks earlier sailors on this route would have encountered skuas, petrels and Sabine's gulls; now, we had a solitary juvenile puffin. Even the gannets had dispersed. Our best hope was a glimpse of the purple sandpipers that hang out on the far-flung rocks to the west; the pelagic summer season was well and truly over.

We were out on the *Sapphire*, a local tripper and wildlife watching boat. To most people, a sapphire is a precious gem: deep blue, flashy and expensive. My *Sapphire* is far more than that. She's still deep blue, flashy and I suspect gloriously expensive; but she has shared my happiest memories with me, while also cradling me through some of my wobblier moments.

By the time we cleared the top of the archipelago, being a rather unseasoned sailor, my face was starting to pale. The gentle, monotonous bobbing and swaying was beginning to induce a familiar weakness in my legs and shakiness in my hands as my stomach quietly protested. I've never actually been seasick, but it's been a close run thing at times. As we rounded the bottom of St Mary's, the largest of the Scilly Isles, we faced the full force of the Atlantic Ocean and things were looking far from peachy.

An 'avian desert' wasn't helping the situation. With nothing to distract the eye and excite the mind, I was beginning to gaze with longing at the cloudy shape of the islands looming to the north, two or three miles away. The frenzied flocks of feeding gannets that had haunted the sea for weeks now quite simply weren't there. Even Bella, the boat's resident spaniel, seemed listless and bored.

Then the cry went up from the boat's captain, Joe: 'Dolphin!'

Sickness forgotten, adrenaline pumping, I snapped into action. As every other passenger ran to port side, scanning the horizon wildly for the tell-tale white water, I threw myself towards the bow of the boat, scrambling over fenders and nearly impaling myself on a fishing rod in the process. No matter – there was time for pain later. Lying stomach-down with one arm wrapped around the railing, I leant forwards (probably quite dangerously, in retrospect) over the side of the boat, breathing hard and waiting.

One second passed, then two, and then:

'Here they come!'

Three, four, five, ten elegant shapes crested the water only a couple of feet below my outstretched fingertips. My head and shoulders lay a good foot beneath the edge of the boat, as I gripped hard with my left arm, stretching the right out towards the surface of the sea; where there had been turquoise only a few seconds before, now powerful and exquisite creatures skimmed the water, sending clouds of mist and spray into our faces as they broke the surface. Deep creamy yellow down the side, stormy blue and slate grey; the classic dolphin shape, smaller than many species but surprisingly large at such close range: the common dolphin.

So near the water, it felt as if we were travelling at considerable speed, although it was probably no more than 10 knots; dolphin after dolphin skimmed the surface, sometimes completely clearing the water in a skilled leap, flicking their tails expertly as they landed to propel themselves forwards. Occasionally one would flip over to lie on its side, and a moment of understanding, or recognition, would pass between us as eye contact was made. This might sound anthropomorphic, but surely this is why there are few human beings who do not smile when they see a dolphin – and not in the patronising way we do with some animals. We see in their gaze an intelligence that is inherently familiar yet completely alien. For us, it is almost inconceivable how creatures can live and prosper beneath the sea; we envy their freedom, their spirit, their obvious love for life, yet we love them for it, too.

It could have been minutes, or hours, that the dolphins rode beneath the bow wave. As they sliced the water the spray caught the setting sunlight, so that it looked like sparks of fire were erupting from the surface. So close to them, I was oblivious to everything else; I knew that there were others around me, but I felt completely alone, almost like I was flying. The only thing I was aware of was Bella, who 'sings' to her ocean friends: a frenzied stream of yelps, yips, barks, snaps, howls and whines combines to make a truly ear-splitting racket. I suspect her canine ears can hear the dolphin's echolocation and she's hopelessly tormented by them. To make it even better, the ocean had by no means calmed, and I was soaked as wave after wave broke over the boat, drenching my head and torso; this only made me feel closer to the dolphins, just out of reach beyond my outstretched finger tips. A soft voice from my partner whispered in my ear: 'Look up.'

I tore my eyes away from the spectacle beneath me. From every direction dolphins were streaming in towards the boat –

countless in number, it seemed. As each pod beneath us peeled off or shot forwards like torpedoes, easily outstripping the boat, another moved in to take their place. It was as if they sensed the sheer, unadulterated joy that was radiating from the front of this little vessel and the bodies both on and below it, separated only by a few inches of air.

Afterwards, it was estimated that there had been as many as 150 individuals around the boat, including many calves. As the autumn progresses the number will increase, sometimes creating 'super pods' that contain many thousands of individuals.

I've seen many photographs and videos of those magical few minutes, and (not to discredit the takers – some were superb) not one of them conveys the entire spectacle. It would be impossible to do so with an image: in this case, words manage it better.

I lay lost in this world for an age, so close and yet so far away from these most wonderful of animals. Gradually, the last of them peeled away, and then with a final flick of the tail, we were alone again.

Standing, shaking, freezing and wet through, I realised that my cheeks were soaked with tears. Salty water mingling with salty water.

Lucy McRobert, 2016

Oct[ober] 21st. 1803. Friday Morning. – A drisling Rain. Heavy masses of shapeless Vapour upon the mountains (O the perpetual Forms of Borrodale!) yet it is no unbroken Tale of dull Sadness – slanting Pillars travel across the Lake, at long Intervals – the vaporous mass whitens, in large Stains of Light – on the (Lakeward) ridge of that huge arm chair, of Lowdore, fell a gleam of softest Light, that brought out the rich hues of the late Autumn. – The woody Castle Crag between me & Lowdore is a rich Flower-Garden of Colours, the brightest yellows with the deepest Crimsons and the infinite Shades of Brown & Green, the *infinite* diversity of which blends the whole – so that the brighter colours seem as *colors* upon a ground, not colored Things.

Little wool-packs of white bright vapour rest on different summits & declivities – the vale is narrowed by the mist & cloud – yet thro' the wall of mist you can see into a bason of sunny Light in Borrodale – the Birds are singing in the tender Rain, as if it were the Rain of April, & the decaying Foliage were Flowers & Blossoms. The pillar of Smoke from the Chimney rises up in the Mist, & is just distinguishable from it; & the Mountain Forms in the Gorge of Borrodale consubstantiate with the mist & cloud even as the pillared Smoke/a shade deeper, & a determinate Form. – (Cleared up. the last thin Fleeces on the bathed Fells.)

Samuel Taylor Coleridge, diaries, 1803

There is an air of fulfilment and rest in the landscape and brooding weather of October. It is like a ghost of summer evening all the time; the faint spears of shadow, the sun's shield tarnished and hanging low, and under the trees, instead of shade, pools of their fallen colours. The fields, being mostly stubble, have still the straw-gold light of summer, but the ploughs move there, as in the very afterglow of harvest, and the earth is gradually revealed again that has not been seen since spring. Other men are at work cementing and closing in the gains of the year against the weather turning enemy. The thatcher mounts his ladder many times with his burden of straw, roofing the corn built to be its own storehouse: over the hedge, the spade of the man earthing up the root-clamp is visible at moments; with regular rhythm it appears suddenly, slaps a slab of grey clay upon the straw, and vanished for another, till the long hump is a fort against frost, neatly moated, too, where the earth has been cut out. The hedger is there also, defeating the hedge in its summer attempt to usurp a yard of the field all round; it is still warm enough for shirt-sleeves, working, and he is a summer figure yet. The farmer, with his gun and dog, is walking the stubble for partridges before they get too wild, to prove to himself that he has not lost his aim since January last, nor his dog her nose. As to the city man his tennis-racquet as he takes it down on a summer's evening, his business done, so to the farmer his gun in the evening glow of autumn. He goes out with it, but for survey of his fields as much as to shoot. He never closes both eyes to his job. The eye he doesn't aim with is seeing that another harrowing is necessary here for wheat.

All the harvest the men have been working as one gang in the fields, but now they are apart at different jobs again, working alone all day, many of them, observing different meal-times; labourers having dinner at one, ploughmen at two-thirty; the cheerful fellowship of the summer is over, and its many voices. No coloured pinafores in the fields either, fluttering like blown petals, for the children have gone back to school. There the youngster of thirteen sits immured, learning to spell, but dreaming of how he drove two horses and a loaded wagon in the hot days, which he considers the only work worthy of a man such as he. His teacher finds him obstinate and dull.

Adrian Bell, Silver Ley, *1931*

There are reasons to love every season: the rebirth and renewal of spring; the welcome warmth of summer; the ritualistic parting of winter with the promise of a new year to come. But I think of autumn as the *ne plus ultra* of seasons.

Tendrils of summer heat creep into these months. The change in colour is a world remade. We sense its gradualness, the minimal shifts that quicken until green gives way to amber, then red: nature's traffic lights. I live in a city that's full of parks and tree-lined roads, but to get a real sense of autumn's flux, I make for the Dublin Mountains. When I was growing up my family would go for Sunday drives, the gears straining as the car climbed up towards woods with names like Kilmashogue, Carrickgollogan, Barnaslingan and Slievethoul (*slieve* or *sliabh* is the Irish word for mountain). High above the city, with the sea visible in the distance, the forests were heavy with the weight of change, of imminent abscission. I'd go home with pockets full of pine cones, and fallen leaves to trace onto paper.

I still visit often, even more so in autumn, and I head straight for two forests that are side by side, bisected by a road. Massy's Wood – once home to a grand family dwelling with an icehouse and walled garden – is now in ruins. What has endured is its magnificent trees from all over the world: monkey puzzle, giant sequoia and western hemlock. Oaks rub shoulders with Monterey pine, while beech and cedar race each other to the clouds. Trunk-knotted yews keep company with drooping willows.

A look at Ireland's place names – not just roads or towns, but entire counties – reminds me that so many owe their names to trees. Derry (*Doire*) is an oak grove or wood; Kildare (*Cilldara*) means 'the church of the oak'; and Mayo (*Maigh Eo*) is 'Plain of the yew'. The ancient Celts divided trees into four categories in order of importance: Nobles, Commoners, Lower Division and Bushes. Some folklorists also believe that they used an Ogham calendar of thirteen months to measure time, each represented by a tree. From September to early November, the corresponding species are hazel, apple, elder, yew and pine. All but one (elder) are classified as Noble or 'chieftain' trees, and all five are present up here in the mountains. An arboreal kingdom, the lungs of this land.

At this time of year, the stagnant summer air is replaced with something more kinetic. Perhaps falling leaves add movement to the space around them. For the first time in months, I can smell frost. The days shorten, but the light is brighter: the foliage of spring and summer make for a heavy canopy, but now the sky is revealed as leaves begin to part ways with their branch hosts. Most deciduous trees drop their leaves, but beeches cling to theirs all through the winter. Reluctant to let go, the leaves move along the spectrum from green to gold to copper, until new buds sever the old. I kick through carpets of fallen rust, of purple, carmine and ochre. I wander among shaded moss and fern, breathing in the damp scent that I've always found comforting.

Across the road is Montpelier Hill, and at the top stands the Hell Fire Club, an old stone hunting lodge, dating back to the early 1700s, that has supernatural connections. It was once the destination of my annual school walk, a round trip of 10 miles in summer heat. On the slow trek upwards, we'd pass

St Colmcille's Well, which pre-dates Christianity. Now encased in concrete, it had a metal tumbler on a chain and, parched, we'd scoop up cold mouthfuls of the water, which was said to cure illness. The Hell Fire Club is a spectacular forest, predominately coniferous, of Sitka spruce, larch and noble fir. Each species of pine has uniquely shaped cones: the rose-like larch and the elongated scales of the Sitka. Last winter, the stumps of newly cut trees were like hives on the landscape. Under the Brehon laws of Celtic history, there were penalties for cutting down noble or commoner trees, usually payable in cattle. The Hell Fire land is owned by Coillte, the national forestry organisation (pronounced 'Kweel-cha', meaning 'woods') and I know this is the cycle of life for a tree up here. But the landscape looks scarred, lacking in height, not itself. The soil floor, once needle-strewn, is now littered with broken branches. Logs are piled high, telling concentric stories of each tree's life. It's not the view of my childhood any more, and by counting the circles, I realise that many of these felled trees were saplings when I was young.

I climb upwards, the path punctuated by giant boulders, to what everybody comes here for: a panoramic view of the city: the crescent of Dublin Bay and the tessellated landscape below. The trees are packed more tightly on the hill, and there are warrens of paths. I've often encountered shy sika deer and rabbits, but there are grouse and kestrel too. During the day, you can find yourself alone in this elevated forest, but it's never silent. The wind rushes through hundreds of branches, a hypnotic symphony, reassuring and eerie all at once. The dark nights roll in with Halloween and, in the forest's charcoal depths, it's hard to ignore its supernatural, *Watcher in the Woods* feel. The hills and trees are spooky in the evening gloom.

The Hell Fire Club itself is a favourite haunt of ghost-hunters. Rumoured to be a den of iniquity, it's mired in stories of dark forces and apparitions. When I was a child it was said that if you ran around the house three times and looked through the doorway, you'd see the devil. We'd scare each other with tales of how his cloven hoof betrayed him during a card game. I've been up here at night and while the lights of the city twinkle, the Hell Fire light is opaque. It's hard to see very far in front of you, unless the moon is up. Next to the car park at the bottom of the hill, there used to be a popular restaurant that was supposedly haunted by a black cat with fierce, red eyes. But the supernatural is not just for buildings; there is magic and superstition in birch, hawthorn and rowan, too. In Ireland, people tie ribbons to rag trees (or 'cloonie trees') so that fairies or spirits will grant wishes.

Our history is full of stories of liberty trees, judgement trees, and trees of life and death. It's fitting that Halloween and All Souls Day fall in autumn; two spiritual worlds overlapping, and the sense of a journey coming to an end. The vigour of summer fades and gives way to the first breath of autumn. The gold-brown-red semaphore of branch and leaf in Massy's Wood will soon be gone, waiting for a new palette to arrive in spring. But on the exposed Hell Fire hill, the evergreens will endure through the coming cold months, a patch of colour when there is little left elsewhere. I'll be back there this year, and every autumn, pocketing cones, listening to the wind in the trees and ignoring the devil in the Hell Fire doorway.

Sinéad Gleeson, 2016

Poem in October

It was my thirtieth year to heaven
Woke to my hearing from harbour and neighbour wood
    And the mussel pooled and the heron
            Priested shore
            The morning beckon
With water praying and call of seagull and rook
And the knock of sailing boats on the net webbed wall
    Myself to set foot
           That second
    In the still sleeping town and set forth.

My birthday began with the water-
Birds and the birds of the winged trees flying my name
    Above the farms and the white horses
            And I rose
        In rainy autumn
And walked abroad in a shower of all my days.
High tide and the heron dived when I took the road
        Over the border
          And the gates
    Of the town closed as the town awoke.

A springful of larks in a rolling
Cloud and the roadside bushes brimming with whistling

Blackbirds and the sun of October
　　　　Summery
　　On the hill's shoulder,
Here were fond climates and sweet singers suddenly
Come in the morning where I wandered and listened
　　　To the rain wringing
　　　　Wind blow cold
　　In the wood faraway under me.

Pale rain over the dwindling harbour
And over the sea wet church the size of a snail
　　With its horns through mist and the castle
　　　　Brown as owls
　　　But all the gardens
Of spring and summer were blooming in the tall tales
Beyond the border and under the lark full cloud.
　　　There could I marvel
　　　　My birthday
　　Away but the weather turned around.

It turned away from the blithe country
And down the other air and the blue altered sky
　　Streamed again a wonder of summer
　　　　With apples
　　　Pears and red currants
And I saw in the turning so clearly a child's
Forgotten mornings when he walked with his mother
　　　Through the parables
　　　　Of sun light
　　And the legends of the green chapels

AUTUMN

And the twice told fields of infancy
That his tears burned my cheeks and his heart moved in mine.
   These were the woods the river and sea
        Where a boy
     In the listening
Summertime of the dead whispered the truth of his joy
To the trees and the stones and the fish in the tide.
    And the mystery
      Sang alive
   Still in the water and singing birds.

And there could I marvel my birthday
Away but the weather turned around. And the true
   Joy of the long dead child sang burning
      In the sun.
   It was my thirtieth
Year to heaven stood there then in the summer noon
Though the town below lay leaved with October blood.
   O may my heart's truth
    Still be sung
  On this high hill in a year's turning.

Dylan Thomas, 1946

It is a crisp autumn morning. As I take the footpath across the hills red kites fly overhead, and all around me flaming red dogwood stems blow in the wind. This hidden nature reserve – Grangelands and the Rifle Range in Buckinghamshire – is one of my favourite places to visit.

There's a log by the path, and when I lift it I find myself a child again, fascinated by the wildlife that awaits me. A violet ground beetle scuttles away, flashing its iridescent wing cases. A chocolate-brown centipede crosses the space previously occupied by the wood, terrorising the other invertebrates around it, which retreat into the surrounding undergrowth before I have a chance to get a good look at them. Springtails of every conceivable size and shape crawl, spring and hop around, trying to escape the predatory invertebrates that want to eat them. There are miniature Serengetis like this under most logs, if you take the time to look.

The hills themselves seem inhospitable to insect life at this time of year so I seek shelter in the strips of beech woodland clinging to the top of the slopes. I look under another log and find a snail hunter beetle hunkered down, its long face adapted to fit into snail shells and eat what's inside. This impressive creature squeaks if you pick it up. There is an abundance of dead wood here, from freshly fallen branches to decaying trunks. Even the structure of the decaying wood is diverse. Most of it is infected by white rot, which makes it hold water and become squidgy. Elsewhere is the hard, cubical red rot that starts from the centre of the tree; it contrasts vividly with the white fungal threads which weave together like balls of string that entwine themselves between the wood and the soil below.

I lift up a number of logs and find little, but underneath this next one it's damper and there are slugs, snails and worms. I watch as earthworms slowly burrow their way through the parts of the log that are so decomposed that they almost resemble soil. When I pick up one of the glossy snails the smell of garlic fills the air and clings to my fingers as I discover why some species are called garlic snails. Next is a ferocious leopard slug, which eats other slugs and always impresses me with its size and the intricate pattern of spots down its back. There are slate-grey pill woodlice which have tucked themselves into every nook and cranny, curled up into the tightest balls possible. Few can munch through their outer shell other than the tough-jawed woodlouse spiders, which feed solely upon them.

But dead wood isn't confined to the ground; the best dead wood is standing. There's a gnarled old horse chestnut tree that I visit on most of my walks here, which is rich with wildlife. I find evidence of beetle larvae tunnelling their way through the wood. Before breaking out as adults, these larvae eat the fungi that break down the wood, their exit holes then supporting nesting bees and wasps for years to come. Hoverfly larvae squelch their way through the rot holes created when the tree loses a limb, and next year will emerge as the beautiful adults that float in the wind on a spring day. This ancient tree must have supported thousands of rare invertebrates in its time, and although now partly dead, it will support life for decades to come.

Ryan Clark, 2016

Last Week in October

The trees are undressing, and fling in many places –
On the gray road, the roof, the window-sill –
Their radiant robes and ribbons and yellow laces;
A leaf each second so is flung at will,
Here, there, another and another, still and still.

A spider's web has caught one while downcoming,
That stays there dangling when the rest pass on;
Like a suspended criminal hangs he, mumming
In golden garb, while one yet green, high yon,
Trembles, as fearing such a fate for himself anon.

Thomas Hardy, published 1928

November

Nov. 3.   Men sow wheat: but the land-springs break out in some of the Hartley malm-fields. [Upper Greensand rock.]

Nov. 5.   Gossamer abounds. Vast dew lies on the grass all day, even in the sun.

Nov. 8.   Planted 3 quarters of an hundred more of cabbages to stand the winter: dug-up potatoes; those in the garden large, & fine, those in the meadow small, & rotting.

Nov. 10.   On this day Brother Benjamin quitted South Lambeth, & came to reside at His House at Mareland.

Nov. 12.   Planted in the garden 2 codling-trees, 2 damson-trees, & 22 goose-berry trees, sent me by Bro^r T. W.

Nov. 13.   Mr Ed. White & man brought a good fine young white poplar from his out-let at Newton, & planted it at ye top of Parsons's, slip behind the bench; where it will be ornamental.

Nov. 15.   Timothy comes out.

Nov. 17.   Baker's hill is planted all over with horse-beans, which are grown four or five inches high. They were probably sown by jays; & spring up thro' the grass, or moss. Many were planted there last year, but not in such abundance as now.

Nov. 19.   Water-cresses come in.

Nov. 21. Sent 3 bantam fowls to Miss Reb. White at Mareland, a cock & two pullets.

Nov. 22. Timothy comes forth.

Nov. 24. Saw a squirrel in Baker's Hill: it was very tame. This was probably what Thomas called a pole-cat [See 28 Oct. *supra.*]

Nov. 26. Timothy hides.

Nov. 29. This dry weather enables men to bring in loads of turf, not much damaged: while scores of loads of peat lie rotting in the Forest.

Dec. 1. Thomas started a hare, which lay in her form under a cabbage, in the midst of my garden. It has begun to eat the tops of my pinks in many places. The landsprings, which began to appear, are much abated.

Dec. 2. This dry fit has proved of vast advantage to the kingdom, & by drying & draining the fallows, will occasion the growing of wheat on many hundred of acres of wet, & flooded land, that were deemed to be in a desperate state, & incapable of being seeded this season.

Dec. 4. Timothy is gone under a tuft of long grass, but is not yet buried in the ground.

Dec. 5 Timothy appears, & flies come-out.

Dec. 7. Took down the urns, & shut up the alcove.

Reverend Gilbert White, The Naturalist's Journal, *1792*

Dusk is already filling the wood. Across the valley some Duracell jackdaws yap, and yap.

There was a storm last night. The floor of the wood is a chaos of crashed branches and downed trunks: a Norse god's idea of Pick-up-Sticks. Among the fallen is the beech-by-the-stile, the one I touch every day as I pass.

Touched. Past tense.

Gothic architects likely got their inspiration for cathedral columns from beech. Certainly the beech-by-the-stile supported the sky.

You think of wood, the stuff, as something warm, domestic; it's the dining table, the parquet floor, the rolling pin. But beech trees are as stone-cold hard as pillars.

I was always the supplicant when I greeted the stile beech. It was a reverent touch I gave, not a matey slap on the back.

I look up through the vertiginous gap she left. (Yes, to my mind she was the queen of this four-acre woodland realm.) There is a hole in the roof of the wood. There is a hole in my day.

But onwards. Time and light are failing. I follow the faint ink line of the path as it squiggles between the dulled obstacles of beech, sweet chestnut, hornbeam. A single stick, hidden under the wet sponge of leaves, snaps; the cannon 'boom' around the vast empty chamber of the wood sends pigeons clattering through the tops of the trees.

The naked trees. Every last leaf was stripped off in the storm. In twenty years I cannot remember such a violent undressing. (It was a north, Viking gale.)

Walking quicker now. Dog-trot. To my left, glimpsed between passing trunks, a finger-smear of dying sun.

The more the blindness, the greater the sense of smell. Ah, the full autumn Bisto bouquet comes powering to the nose: mouldering leaves, decaying mushrooms, rusting earth.

I'm just skirting the little dingle, where the yellow marsh marigolds bloom in spring, when the woodcock explodes from under my foot. An avian IED. I shout out unmanfully in the silence. Luckily, in a wood on the far edge of Herefordshire there is no one to hear me scream.

Once, woodcock were common. Some still nest locally, over on Ewyas Harold Common, but this was an autumn migrant, borne on the November gale.

When God made the dumpy woodcock He was in the same whimsical frame of mind as when He cobbled up the platypus. Although the size of a hand, the woodcock has an improbable 3-inch stiletto stuck on its face. The bird books label the woodcock's brown-and-white, flecked-and-striped plumage as an example of 'crypsis'; 'magick' would be closer to the mark. Only the curlew, snipe and nightjar possess more effective camouflage. Woodcock are seamless with their surroundings. They are the leaf blown through the beech grove, the shimmer in the larch. And the rotten elder stump beside the path.

Softly, softly now.

I take the right fork through the birch and reach the pond, with its year-weary, spavined reeds.

No wild duck tonight. The only tenant around is the moorhen; she paddles away, invisible on the black surface except for the travelling, replicating V of her bow wave.

What's in a name? An archaeology of meaning. This is Pond Wood, named for its medieval piscatorial pool. Except for some fat abboty carp, the fish are long gone. For the last two hundred years the pool has been a drinking resource for thirsty cattle, mine included.

I pause for a minute, until the woodland air fades to pure TV monotone grey. With all colour gone, there are only degrees of shadow, of nuance, of insolidity.

The wolf-light.

I can hear the cattle moving; the crackle of branches under hooves, the slow drum beat of moving, massive beasts. It is some sound, I tell you; it is the sound of aurochs in wildwood.

There they are, out in the towers of oak, four longhorn cows, prehistoric shapes plodding up to the top of the wood. To the sanctuary of high ground. There they will lie in a ragged circle watching for the sabre-toothed tigers of bovine nightmares.

Longhorns have proper bicycle-handlebar horns. Longhorns, indeed. They come from the old time, and are no strangers to death amid the trees.

And I am the killer in the wood. A few, shallow, regularising breaths . . . I press off the safety catch of the Baikal .410 shotgun, and slip into the noise shadow of the cattle. When I was a child I read BB's *Brendon Chase*, his adventure story about the Hensman boys who lived feral in the forest, shooting for the pot. This is *Brendon Chase* for grown-ups. And why not? I manage the wood for wildlife; should not wildlife in return provide me with a meal?

The cattle shuffle under the ballerina-arm of the Dead Oak, on which rests the silhouette of a cock pheasant . . .

The flash-blast of the shotgun rips the wood apart. The cattle trumpet alarms. The tawny owl cries out.

The pheasant plunges head first, tail streaming behind. A black comet falling to earth.

In the poker game of life and death we all have our tics. The pheasant had roosted on the same branch for a month, each night dropping his white guano onto the ground.

As I pick up the pheasant, a gap comes in the clouds. The north star shines brightly, more brightly than usual.

John Lewis-Stempel, 2016

The fox appears out of nowhere. One moment Darsham Marshes is ours alone and the next it is his – slinking over the saturated ground with a fluidity matched only by the movement of his shoulders.

The sun has been Scandinavian-low all day but now it is creeping closer towards the treeline. Wave after wave of autumnal light breaks over a Suffolk landscape criss-crossed by the dark veins of dykes, adding golden fire to the big dog fox's flame-red coat.

My wife and I hardly dare to breathe. Although the fox is some distance away we can clearly see his broad head and the distinctive vulpine mask of his face. His neck is already cloaked in a thick mane of winter fur.

I realise with a shock that this is probably the first time I have really seen a fox. There have, of course, been previous encounters. But whether skittering across a road away from headlights or standing with burning yellow eyes on my old Brighton rubbish bin, these were always meetings where I had rudely blundered into the fox's routine – had crashed in on nature – and been rewarded with only the briefest glimpse of russet red and a disappearing rump.

This is different. We had been waiting for the barn owls who regularly ghost across this marsh to hunt and, as such, we had been still, silent, and relatively hidden from view. But also, I notice with relief, we are upwind and there's little chance the fox will catch the scent of the goose-pimpled and muddy tourists loitering in his terrain.

The fox is now skirting down a hedge heading for a copse about 100 metres away. He looks confident, relaxed even, ignoring the ratcheting call of a blackbird and the bovine stares coming from the cattle that graze this marsh.

Then suddenly, as if a whistle has been blown, he stops. Ears twitching he drops into a half crouch, his white-tagged brush held straight behind him. At first I think he has somehow sensed us; has heard our whispered adulation, our Goretex rustle or the plastic pop of a binocular lens cap. But then he's off again, still looking ahead at the same patch of trees, trotting with assurance and stealth over the marsh and out of view.

We grin excitedly at each other and instinctively move to follow him, to continue to be part of his world. But the path around the wetland is heavy going. The cattle here clearly hate getting their feet wet too and their passage has churned much of the track into shin-deep mud. In places they have left pot-like casts of their lower legs.

Changing tack, we try to emulate the fox, stepping off the path and on to the saturated wetland. We jump towards clumps of taller grass, hoping their roots will be strong enough to hold us. But with each clumsy leap the dark water sponges out of the ground and over the tops of our boots. We are getting nowhere fast.

Retracing our steps we hit the path and decide to strike out for home and dinner. From behind us in the darkening copse, comes an explosion of noise – the helicoptering whir of wings and a hoarse alarm call. Two hen pheasants break cover, but the noise continues.

The fox, too, has dinner on his mind.

Matt Gaw, 2016

Lapwings

They were everywhere. No. Just God or smoke
is that. They were the backdrop to the road,

my parents' home, the heavy winter fields
from which they flashed and kindled and uprode

the air in dozens. I ignored them all.
'What are they?' 'Oh – peewits – ' Then a hare flowed,

bounded the furrows. Marriage. Child. I roamed
round other farms. I only knew them gone

when, out of a sad winter, one returned.
I heard the high mocked cry 'Pee – wit', so long

cut dead. I watched it buckle from vast air
to lure hawks from its chicks. That time had gone.

Gravely, the parents bobbed their strip of stubble.
How had I let this green and purple pass?

Fringed, plumed heads (full name, the crested plover)
fluttered. So crowned cranes stalk Kenyan grass.

AUTUMN

Then their one child, their anxious care, came running,
squeaked along each furrow, dauntless, daft.

Did I once know the story of their lives,
do they migrate from Spain? or coasts' cold run?

And I forgot their massive arcs of wing.
When their raw cries swept over, my head spun

With all the brilliance of their black and white
As though you cracked the dark and found the sun.

Alison Brackenbury, 2013

The valley was ablaze with the colour of brilliant decay as the cycle of winter began with a fresh palette. Crows blown like black handkerchiefs from a funeral feast into the tangled treetops exchanged shrill chatter there, a running commentary on all that was happening around them. Everything was in vibrant flux. All was decay.

The best of the heather had already been clipped and picked for the making of besoms. The longest branches and thickest clusters had been cut to size and bundled around a stouter pole – always willow – by those solitary bodgers and gamekeepers' wives who had gained the landowner's permission, and who sang the same song as they worked at home with blade and cord, always sung to a melody that followed a descending glissando of notes:

Buy broom buzzems,
Buy them when they're new,
Fine heather bred uns,
Better never grew.

The heather's flowers too had been taken and set to boil in pots or hung to dry in clusters from mullions and over inglenooks, their mauve colourings turning darker with the darkening of shortened days bookended by nights that birthed new mythologies from old fears.

The heather of the Calder Valley was burned at the behest of the few. Men unseen. Landowners who rarely walked the land they owned, let alone lived on. These were men from the cities, who spent their days away paving turnpikes and building mills. Sinking canals and striking deals. Buying and selling. Traders. Sons of the empire. Men for whom too much was never enough.

Their estate work was done by land managers and it was these who took the heather plant and used its gruit for brewing the ale that filled their master's bow-roofed cellars, while others used the barren moorland spaces for housing hives for their honey-making. Sheep and deer grazed up there and grouse nested in it too, but mainly the heather was used for the dying of the wools.

The slow smoke drifted down to settle on the houses of those weavers and land workers who lived in the hamlets and farmsteads that sat below the moor line. The scent of it was the latest subtle signal to mark autumn's tightening grip on the land.

The incoming season meant death and soon the trees were to become bone-like, and their leaves would gather in drifts down in the lanes, and the animals were already gorging themselves before winter inevitably announced itself in a famine of everything but frost and fire and flickering candles below the patch-blackened shapes of moorland that saw shouting men with their brooms and beaters and handkerchiefs tied tight around their faces from late September.

Come April the pitch-coloured rectangles of burnt heather shadows would be dotted with the white fingers of new shoots peeping through, though as this summer past withered and died, slowly curling in on itself into crisp husks and falling skeletons, the very thought of next spring's re-birth seemed one beyond realisation for most in the valley, an impossibility, a wild, fanciful vision of the deluded.

Benjamin Myers, extract from The Gallows Pole, *publishing 2017*

The Stag

While the rain fell on the November woodland shoulder of Exmoor
While the traffic jam along the road honked and shouted
Because the farmers were parking wherever they could
And scrambling to the bank-top to stare through the tree-fringe
Which was leafless,
The stag ran through the private forest.

While the rain drummed on the roofs of the parked cars
And the kids inside cried and daubed their chocolate and fought
And mothers and aunts and grandmothers
Were a tangle of undoing sandwiches and screwed-round gossiping
    heads
Steaming up the windows,
The stag loped through his favourite valley.

While the blue horseman down in the boggy meadow
Sodden nearly black, on sodden horses,
Spaced as at a military parade,
Moved a few paces to the right and a few to the left and felt rather
    foolish
Looking at the brown impassable river,
The stag came over the last hill of Exmoor.

While everybody high-kneed it to the bank top all along the road

AUTUMN

Where steady men in oilskins were stationed with binoculars,
And the horsemen by the river galloping anxiously this way and that
And the cry of hounds came tumbling invisibly with their echoes
down through the draggle of trees,
Swinging across the wall of dark woodland,
The stag dropped in to strange country.

And turned at the river
Hearing the hound-pack smash the undergrowth, hearing the bell-
note
Of the voice carried all others,
Then while the limbs all cried different directions to his lungs, which
only wanted to rest,
The blue horsemen on the bank opposite
Pulled aside the camouflage of their terrible planet.

And the stag doubled back weeping and looking for home up a valley
and down a valley
While the strange trees struck him and the brambles lashed him,
And the strange earth came galloping after him carrying the loll-
tongued hounds to fling all over him
And his heart became just a club beating his ribs and his own hooves
shouted with hounds' voices,
And the crowd on the road got back into their cars
Wet-through and disappeared.

Ted Hughes, 1976

Frost crackles underfoot as I walk through the meadow of Gilfach Farm. It's not early, but it feels as if the trees and mountains are still asleep. Above me, the sky is pierced by the echoing call of circling buzzard.

More gentle is the sound of the river as it slips beneath the bridge, bubbling over the stones. I've spotted a dipper here before, standing proud in the middle of the water, ready for dinner. But it's the fish I'm here for today. I've heard that it's possible to see leaping salmon, a spectacle of nature that I've witnessed on screen but not in person. I'm full of anticipation, but caution myself not to get too excited in case nothing happens.

Strolling through the meadow, I think back to summer here: butterflies dancing between flowers, and the song of migrant birds filling the woods. How different it feels in autumn. It's cold too, and I shiver despite my layers. The river becomes louder as I walk along, and I know I'm approaching the waterfall.

I take my place on the wooden platform by the cascading water, nodding in greeting to my fellow watchers.

To see a salmon, patience is needed. I spend over an hour on the platform. Despite the cold, it's a soothing experience. It is easy to become hypnotised when watching the water. Every splash seems different, but it's all part of the same rhythm that I find myself getting drawn into. My eyes feel as if they are glazing over, mesmerised by the flow.

Suddenly a flash of brown among the white foam, impossibly swimming upstream against the water. A salmon! My heart is in my mouth, then sinks as the salmon fails on this jump and falls back downstream into the swirling pool below. It isn't long before it tries again, and inside I'm cheering it on, willing it to complete the leap and get over this hurdle. It surely must. It has leapt over so many other hurdles in its journey to this point, surely it can manage a few more to get beyond the waterfall. Again it fails.

But I believe in this fish; it can make the jump. It has battled against the oceans, avoided capture by prey and by humans, found its way back to the river of its birth and swum this far up already; it will surely get up this waterfall with ease.

Eventually, with an enormous leap, it succeeds. Clearing the foaming water, its whole body flies through the air into the next pool. There is now one less jump needed before the top of the waterfall is reached, and then it will be home to breed. I almost cheer out loud. I don't, though, as there are other people about and I don't want to seem too mad.

I have seen plenty of leaping salmon since that first one, but each time the thrill is as great as I watch them battle the water in order to create new life further upstream.

Megan Shersby, 2016

Fieldfares, when they arrive early and in great abundance in autumn, foreshew hard winter, which has probably set in, in the regions from which they have come. They usually come in November.

Thomas Furly Forster, The Pocket Encyclopaedia
of Natural Phenomena, *published 1827*

November

The landscape sleeps in mist from morn till noon;
And, if the sun looks through, 'tis with a face
Beamless and pale and round, as if the moon,
When done the journey of her nightly race,
Had found him sleeping, and supplied his place.
For days the shepherds in the fields may be,
Nor mark a patch of sky – blindfold they trace,
The plains, that seem without a bush or tree,
Whistling aloud by guess, to flocks they cannot see.

The timid hare seems half its fears to lose,
Crouching and sleeping 'neath its grassy lair,
And scarcely startles, tho' the shepherd goes
Close by its home, and dogs are barking there;
The wild colt only turns around to stare
At passer by, then knaps his hide again;
And moody crows beside the road, forbear
To fly, tho' pelted by the passing swain;
Thus day seems turn'd to night, and tries to wake in vain.

The owlet leaves her hiding-place at noon,
And flaps her grey wings in the doubling light;
The hoarse jay screams to see her out so soon,
And small birds chirp and startle with affright;

AUTUMN

Much doth it scare the superstitious wight,
Who dreams of sorry luck, and sore dismay;
While cow-boys think the day a dream of night,
And oft grow fearful on their lonely way,
Fancying that ghosts may wake, and leave their graves by day.

Yet but awhile the slumbering weather flings
Its murky prison round – then winds wake loud;
With sudden stir the startled forest sings
Winter's returning song – cloud races cloud,
And the horizon throws away its shroud,
Sweeping a stretching circle from the eye;
Storms upon storms in quick succession crowd,
And o'er the sameness of the purple sky
Heaven paints, with hurried hand, wild hues of every dye.

At length it comes among the forest oaks,
With sobbing ebbs, and uproar gathering high;
The scared, hoarse raven on its cradle croaks,
And stockdove-flocks in hurried terrors fly,
While the blue hawk hangs o'er them in the sky. –
The hedger hastens from the storm begun,
To seek a shelter that may keep him dry;
And foresters low bent, the wind to shun,
Scarce hear amid the strife the poacher's muttering gun.

The ploughman hears its humming rage begin,
And hies for shelter from his naked toil;
Buttoning his doublet closer to his chin,
He bends and scampers o'er the elting soil,

While clouds above him in wild fury boil,
And winds drive heavily the beating rain;
He turns his back to catch his breath awhile,
Then ekes his speed and faces it again,
To seek the shepherd's hut beside the rushy plain.

The boy, that scareth from the spiry wheat
The melancholy crow – in hurry weaves,
Beneath an ivied tree, his sheltering seat,
Of rushy flags and sedges tied in sheaves,
Or from the field a shock of stubble thieves.
There he doth dithering sit, and entertain
His eyes with marking the storm-driven leaves;
Oft spying nests where he spring eggs had ta'en,
And wishing in his heart 'twas summer-time again.

Thus wears the month along, in checker'd moods,
Sunshine and shadows, tempests loud, and calms;
One hour dies silent o'er the sleepy woods,
The next wakes loud with unexpected storms;
A dreary nakedness the field deforms –
Yet many a rural sound, and rural sight,
Lives in the village still about the farms,
Where toil's rude uproar hums from morn till night
Noises, in which the ears of Industry delight.

At length the stir of rural labour's still,
And Industry her care awhile foregoes;
When Winter comes in earnest to fulfil
His yearly task, at bleak November's close,

AUTUMN

And stops the plough, and hides the field in snows;
When frost locks up the stream in chill delay,
And mellows on the hedge the jetty sloes,
For little birds – then Toil hath time for play,
And nought but threshers' flails awake the dreary day.

John Clare, 1827

On one of the highest chalk hills in England, within the ramparts of an Iron Age hill fort and miles from any water, there is a strange autumnal gathering of birds. They arrive each November and stay till March. They are not there by day and come in after dark, pitching in among the sheep and the brown hares, among the whitened grasses and the speared sentries of brown thistle. Here, in the dead of night, it is possible to spot dozens of snipe, golden plover, woodcock and, astonishingly, ruff.

Undisturbed scrubby fields of tussocky grass are a rarity in the farmed landscape. They represent small islands; isolated sanctuaries. Encircled by massive earthworks, this domed 974 ft (297 m) almost-mountain must seem as a beacon to hard-pressed birds.

Full dark. As we walk out on to the hill, there is a frisson of excitement as we hear the melancholy whistle of golden plover and the piping of snipe: the waders are here.

We have seen more than forty snipe, tucked along the parallel wheel ruts of the old cart track. Around them, feeding and more widely scattered, are as many woodcock. We've also seen jack snipe here. You'd think they would be sitting ducks to creeping foxes, yet many pairs of eyes, a shrill whistle and a nervous disposition stand them in good stead.

They come to roost and feed on this bleakest, most exposed place. As our eyes adjust to the night, the ramparts, ditch and drop are as a solid silhouette above the tenuous lights of the distant town. The stars wheel and turn above. I can hear redwings calling *seeip* as they go over. The chill in the air deepens and grows damp as the temperature reaches the dew point and it begins to freeze.

Golden plover run along, calling sweetly to each other – but most of them are out on the big arable fields in larger flocks. The snipe are alert and adept at keeping completely still until you are right on top of them, when they explode from the earth with a screechy *scaarp*. Their camouflage of brown, cream and tawny-gold streaked feathers mimics a fold of tussocky grass perfectly. Often, we only know they're there when the big lamp glints off an eye. (And then, sometimes, a camouflaged body does not form and we find we're looking intently at a bead of dew on the grass.)

The woodcock are less easily spooked. I manage to creep up on one, my friend keeping the lamp indirectly on it, so that the bird remains on the shallow edge of the pool of light. I get about as close as it's possible to get to a woodcock in the grass until I am kneeling beside it. It continues to feed, pushing its incomprehensibly long bill into the ground as if it were a ponderous sewing-machine needle. It leaves little stitch holes in its wake.

I can see astonishing detail in its cryptic, complex dead-leaf-and-grass plumage, as well as the bump of the sensitive, worm-seeking tip to its bill. Its bright, watchful eye is set far back in its head for 360° vision. My eyes water and sting with the effort of not blinking, but I cannot take them off the bird. It bobs rhythmically as it walks – almost crawls – along, waddling slightly. It is a piece of turf come alive, a jigsaw piece of grass that gets up to walk alongside me and the lamp trembling in my friend's hand. The woodcock is a creature absolutely inseparable from its environment.

We go quietly along until we see the fourth wader we'd hoped was here. The ruff took us completely by surprise when we first saw them. We disbelieved our own eyes, seeking reassurances from each other, knowing them to be rare and unlikely up here.

It took several nights and much leafing through books and spending time online to be certain, but they are here in plain view. Out of breeding season, ruff are unremarkable, long-legged brown waders. Stockier than the snipe, they have long necks, small heads and a shorter, faintly downcurved bill. Their demeanour and movement as apologetic as a muntjac's.

In flight, these ostensibly similar birds are testing our ID skills tonight, and I'm a beat behind my companion. The snipe fly fast, calling and zig-zagging on narrow, boomerang wings, white under-carriages to the frosty ground. If we are lucky, a diagnostic white wing-edge gleams in the beam. Bulkier woodcock go straight up, just once, to hover like winged angels before landing close by. But the ruff are still a new species for us both, complicating and thrilling the night. Their flight is slower, lower and more hesitant.

For several nights now, we have been up to see them, guessing and speculating at where they go in the day. It is both wildly exciting and poignant. There is an air of 'last chance to see' about these waders, and discovering them here brings a particular sense of responsibility.

Because there are plans to mow, tidy and intensively graze this field, to remove the scrub thorns from the ramparts and within. It hurts. What impact will it have on these birds people either do not know about, do not care for, or do not believe are here? But there is a line I must toe and not cross. This is a working farm and my family are tenants. My co-discoverer is both employee and tenant. On the nights when I'm not up there, I hatch plans and cannot sleep.

Nicola Chester, 2016

Two hours and forty-two minutes. A reasonable time. Not the quickest by any means, but this was not a day for haste; today was meant for reflection, it was to be savoured and made the most of. It was the last good day of the year.

A hundred or so acres to survey around the London Wetland Centre. Reclaimed reservoirs and managed habitat nestled against the Thames, passed by university rowing crews and pleasure boats. Their shouts and cries accompany any trip down the remote east path, masking my swearing and cursing as the vegetation, grown wild as the year progressed, fought to bar the way ahead. Heathrow-bound jets and helicopter traffic rumbled above me. Over- and underground train whistles mixed with sirens pierced the air. In summer these sounds competed with chattering martins, screaming swifts and the rattling of warblers who filled the reeds and also called this place their home; without them the sky seems quiet and chilling.

I had shied away from the centre for years, displaying the London indifference to any attraction; it'll be there next week, or the week after . . . It can wait. That first visit – the year now hazy, but the clear, cold day not – a council-estate life forgotten within moments of entering. The concrete crumbling on each visit, allowing room to learn and see new things. Walks, talks, events, I went to them all, gradually discovering more. I bought binoculars and the long forgotten joy of photography bloomed again.

As others looked skyward, I looked down and saw basking lizards. I would lie close to them for minutes, hours at times, to take pictures and establish some level of trust. More than once a passer-by would think I had met some terrible fate as I lay still on the ground, enquiring if I was OK. My solitary world was opened up, the fascinating little animals my release, talking gently to them as I took portraits.

I can't remember exactly how, or even when, I ended up with a name badge. I had fallen in with staff and volunteers due to my frequent visits and knowledge of lizard locations. I dabbled with some events and helped out where I could, overcoming my dislike of humans. One day I chanced upon friends armed with a clipboard: 'We're doing a reptile survey, want to join us?' They may even have explained the risks – nettles, biting ants, mud, brambles, electric fences, cows and more – but I had heard all I needed.

A map showed the refugia dotted around the centre: thirty-eight pairs of them, one tin, the other a square of roofing felt. They were mainly far from prying eyes, over-inquisitive hands and disturbance. Their positions soon became fixed in my mind, the routes automatic, the paths my own. A lone meandering to find reptiles – and myself, at times.

The season started in April, with weekly surveys until the end of June, and had begun again in September. Throughout the year, weather beat the felts and tins down; they became blockaded by nettles and brambles, blanketed by leaves and fallen fruit. Two survey points were gone now, choked by thick, thorny vines streaked with ballooned gossamer, full autumnal black fruits shining in the low sun, taunting, waiting for early winter migrants.

Regulars were missing too. That dark female slow worm under E1A, curled in a hollow every week until one visit when the survey sheet was empty and has remained so. I hope she is OK.

Then there was the long girl under the tin at A2. Her tail intact, unlike many on site. She was swollen and lethargic after the summer break, heavier the following survey and last week she was gone. The felt next to her regular spot was lifted to reveal a mass of bronze and metallic black strands of spaghetti, curled together, making a count tricky. Staying immobile long enough for us to spot nine of them and then bursting in every direction for the grass, proving one of the first things I was taught about these reptiles: they're neither slow nor worms. This week the number was up to eleven, with five more under the tin, but still without the mother. She may have headed to winter quarters now, or to feed up beforehand. The young were on their own from the start, scale replicas of the parents, tiny blinking eyes and notched tongue, pure instinct driving them. I always hoped to see these new arrivals the following year, to greet them after their first hibernation. I worried about broods born so late.

Some of the common lizards had shown up only in the last weeks too; clusters of deep bronze, jewels, not much larger than a thumbnail, huddled on sun-warmed wooden bridges, posts and benches, blissfully ignored by passers-by who, like me years before, didn't know the little creatures existed, let alone in London. My fingers were crossed for them in the months ahead.

Grass snake hatchlings had been seen in early September. Tiny, no thicker than a bootlace, full of tricks already; playing dead, musking and hissing. A few inches of comical theatrics that would grow to be the UK's largest reptile. Now, the scent of their musk remained a heady memory to last through the months of hibernation, to be refreshed in the spring. The smell would stay on your skin for days, no matter how hard you scrubbed.

The picnic area provided a good spot to finish the paperwork, a tin and felt hidden nearby. The benches quiet now, allowing time to write and think of past months as well as those ahead, when there would be nowhere to hide.

The pen hesitated. The numbers double, triple checked and then totalled.

In the office, the folder was closed for the last time this year. A stack of survey sheets, crumpled in places, wrinkled from rain, streaked with mud, were the evidence of all the hours and miles walked. The name badge removed. It was hibernation time.

Laurence Arnold, 2016

Murmuration

You are speaking in a flight of starlings,
in words that have the sheen of metal, a flash
of green or purple, an iridescence
on your tongue.

Starling words, once spoken, fly up
in swarms through a calm sky, through
the long light of evening,
and can never be unspoken or forgotten.

Imtiaz Dharker, 2014

Two autumns in a row, hares came and bred in the overgrown field in front of the cottage, around my well. Hares were not at all common here; they didn't like the closely cropped improved grassland of the hill farms, and although hares are active in the daytime and therefore easier to see than most mammals, sometimes weeks would go by without my seeing a single one. They are tough creatures that live out in the open all seasons, all weathers. They don't rely on burrows or nests for shelter and protection but on their ability to outrun predators. And they are fast; if they lived in town they could easily break the speed limit. As a child I would see them in large numbers when I walked on the marshes. In spring I would make a point of going to look for them so I could watch them boxing: the traditional spectacle of the mad March hares. At that time their fights were thought to be between the males, known as jacks, competing for the attention of the females, known as jills; now it is believed that it is actually the females, to our eyes indistinguishable from the males, fighting off the premature or unwanted attentions of the males. But here the jack was in no danger of getting his crown broken. The problem for the females here was not fighting off unwanted suitors but finding a mate, any mate, in the first place.

Hares can breed at any time of year, and the young leverets have to be as hardy as the adults, for they are left in a form, a hollow in the grass that offers no more protection than the bare scrape of the nest of a wader. Their defence from predators is to stay very, very still until they have no alternative but to run.

183

The fields of sheep-grazing didn't offer enough cover for them, but the field around my well was becoming visibly more and more overgrown year on year, as bracken spread from the edge of Penlan Wood, along with banks of sedge where the field was boggy, and nettles and thistles in the drier ground around the rocky remains of Penlan Farm. Sheep still passed through, but the field was growing steadily more marginal and unappetizing for them, and steadily more attractive for wildlife. I had no idea how many leverets were in the field, for they were all hidden in separate spots, for safety's sake, but for a whole month of each of those two successive autumns it seemed as though whenever I walked down to my well, little hares would explode from every stand of nettles, every clump of sedge.

They didn't all make it. One year, on the twenty-foot slab of exposed rock beside my fruit tree, where the mosses and liverworts grew, I found the bloody stump of a young hare's hind leg. Dropped there by a buzzard, I supposed, or perhaps by hawk. I was fairly sure it had been carried there rather than killed there, as there was no sign of plucked fur, or any other remains. Just that one solitary paw. The next year, I found a skinned leveret on the track in front of the cottage. The skin was inside out, with the fur facing inwards like the wool on a sheepskin coat. The head had been eaten, but all four paws were snapped off and still attached. It was a neat job, the work of a badger, I thought, rather than a fox. Badgers didn't often approach this close to the cottage – only once had I gone out at night and surprised one at my fence – but this drama had taken place right outside my window, in the deep darkness while I slept, and I had not been disturbed.

One late-autumn day I opened a back door to fetch some water, and there was a young hare sat on my back step. Save for the twitching of its nose, it froze in position as if I had surprised it as it was about to knock. It was already the size of a full-grown rabbit, and its black-tipped ears were longer than any rabbit's would ever be. I stood there and waited for it to flush. After a while I began to doubt that it would, and squatted down to its level for a closer look, eye to eye. It stared back at me apparently unconcerned, chewing silently, with bulging eyes that were such a rich golden colour they were almost orange, with black depths like the keyhole of a door to another world. I tried to imagine what might be going on in its mind, whether it might be ill or injured, and considered what might happen if I tried to pick it up. It seemed like a risky survival strategy, to trust in your camouflage when you are sitting on a doorstep, and I wondered if its sibling had done the same when it had been caught out by a badger on my track. As I touched the little hare, it burst into life and raced away at incredible speed, turning on a pin at the corner of the cottage. I dashed after it and was in time to see it clear my drystone wall, fence and all: a perfect arc of perhaps twenty feet. The next day the young hares had gone from my front field, scattered. They were so close to adulthood now, ready to begin their wandering, and I wouldn't see a single hare again until Christmas.

Neil Ansell, Deep Country: Five Years in the Welsh Hills, *2011*

Redbreast or Robbin Redbreast *Sylvia rubicolay*, migrates from the groves and thickets towards the habitation of man in November, and in the frost of the hybernal season comes close to our windows, and even our firesides, when it can find entrance, in search of food.

Thomas Furly Forster, The Pocket Encyclopaedia of Natural Phenomena, *published 1827*

Warming

The seasons' course seems strange to me,
more strange than I remember.
Wild flowers bloom unseasonably:
primroses in November.

The young pretend to blame us all.
Well, youth's a great dissembler:
May was forever, I recall,
and there was no November.

These days I'll take what Nature sends
to hoard for dour December:
a glow of warmth as autumn ends;
primroses in November.

David Gwilym Anthony, 2012

Author Biographies

Nick Acheson grew up in wellies, watching bog bush-crickets in North Norfolk. A year spent in the Camargue during his degree inspired him to seek wilder landscapes and for ten glorious years he lived in Bolivia. Since returning to the UK he has worked the world over, from Arctic tundras to the Antarctic. He proudly works closely with Norfolk Wildlife Trust, for whom he regularly features in local press and media.

Jane Adams grew up in an overcrowded London suburb with an unexplained love of all things wild. It took forty years before her passion properly surfaced after moving to an old house on the south coast with a rambling, wild garden. Now a self-confessed middle-aged wildlife nerd, her interests include photography, social media, writing, trail running and nature conservation. @wildlifestuff

Neil Ansell left London to live alone in the remote wilds of the Welsh country-side without electricity, gas, water, transport or a phone. After five years of semi-isolation, he wrote *Deep Country* (2011), recounting his experiences and reflecting on man's relationship with nature. He is now an award-winning journal-ist, working with the BBC, *Guardian* and *New Statesman* among others.

David Gwilym Anthony, author of three books of poetry including *Passing through the Woods* (Matador, 2012), was born in Ffestiniog, North Wales, brought up in Hull and studied modern history at St Catherine's College, Oxford. He lives in Stoke Poges, Buckinghamshire, near the churchyard where Thomas Gray, author of *Elegy in a Country Churchyard*, is buried.

Laurence Arnold has an affinity for the misunderstood creatures in nature and escapes the day job by volunteering to count bats and reptiles at the London Wet-land Centre and eels on the Hogsmill. He enjoys photography and using old film cameras, cycling, pretending to be Basque and once appeared on *Vic Reeves' Big Night Out*.

Paul Ashton is currently head of Biology at Edge Hill University. A native of Lancashire, previous study and employment saw him happily exiled to Scotland and Norfolk before returning to the North West. For over twenty years he has striven to fire an enthusiasm for plants, evolution and conservation in his students, a mission he is still energetically engaged in.

Louise Baker is the granddaughter of a naturalist, a mother to two small, curious boys, and a freelance writer with an interest in childhood and the natural world, and how the two collide. As well as writing for a variety of clients Louise volunteers her services to the Derbyshire Wildlife Trust, and keeps a blog, 'The Many Adventures of Lexi and Tubs', to document the family's wild adventures.

Ginny Battson is a professional nature and landscape photographer with a lifelong love of wildlife, especially that of woodlands and watery habitats. Her passions include environmental ethics, ecoliteracy and being a mother. She enjoys walking, wading, observing and writing her blog seasonalight.wordpress.com. She lived in the US and New Zealand before returning to live in Wales.

Adrian Bell (d. 1980) was a Suffolk farmer and journalist who wrote over twenty-five ruralist books, including *Corduroy* (1930) *Silver Ley* (1931) and *The Cherry Tree* (1932), which together form his farm trilogy. He was the first person to compile the now legendary *Times* crossword, setting over 5,000 puzzles and helping to develop the cryptic clue style.

Kate Blincoe is a nature-loving mother of two and freelance writer for publications such as the *Guardian*. She is the author of *The No-Nonsense Guide to Green Parenting* and is never happier than when exploring the countryside with her family.

Alison Brackenbury is the author of seven collections of poetry, for which she has been the recipient of several awards. Born in Lincolnshire, she was educated at Oxford and now lives in Gloucestershire.

Will Burns was brought up in Buckinghamshire. He is the Poet-in-Residence at Caught by the River and in 2014 was named as a Faber New Poet. His pamphlet was Number 10 in that series.

Brian Carter (d. 2015) was a Devon-based author, artist and conservation columnist with a deep affection for the landscape and wildlife of his home county.

Many of his writings featured his beloved Dartmoor as backdrop, including *A Black Fox Running* (1981) and *Jack: A Novel* (1986).

Jo Cartmell is a lifelong naturalist with a special interest in water voles and wildflower meadows. She runs the Twitter accounts @WaterVole and @NearbyWild and also blogs for nearbywild.org.uk about her local wildlife.

Nicola Chester writes about the wildlife she finds wherever she is, mostly roaming the North Wessex Downs, where she lives with her husband and three children. She has written professionally for over a decade. Nicola is particularly passionate about engaging people with nature and how language can communicate the thrill of wild experiences. You can read her blog here: nicolachester. wordpress.com

Horatio Clare is the bestselling author of two memoirs, *Running for the Hills* and *Truant*; three books of nature and travel, *A Single Swallow*, *Down to the Sea in Ships*, and *Orison for a Curlew*; a novella, *The Prince's Pen*; an anthology, *Sicily Through Writers' Eyes*, and most recently a novel for children, *Aubrey and the Terrible Yoot*, a *Sunday Times* children's book of the year.

John Clare (d. 1864) was the son of a farm labourer who went on to produce some of English poetry's best works on the countryside, rural life and nature. Known as The Northamptonshire Peasant Poet in his time, a sense of alienation and disruption became themes of this work, such as 'I Am' (1848).

Ryan Clark is a twenty-two-year-old professional ecologist based in Buckinghamshire. A lifelong wildlife recorder, he enjoys going for walks in the Chilterns, recording and photographing wildlife. His main passions are plants and pollinators, especially solitary bees. He loves sharing his passion for British wildlife with others and regularly blogs at ryanclarkecology.wordpress.com

William Cobbett (d. 1835) was a farmer, radical politician and perhaps the greatest pamphleteer of his generation. He was the editor of the *Political Register,* which published every week from 1802 until the year of his death, and forms an invaluable record of the social life of his age as well as its political turmoil. As an author he is best known for his book *Rural Rides* (1830).

Samuel Taylor Coleridge (d. 1834) was a poet, literary critic and philosopher whose joint publication with William Wordsworth, *Lyrical Ballads* (1798), is credited with marking the beginning of the Romantic period in English poetry. A member of the Lake Poets, some of his most famous works include 'The Rime of the Ancient Mariner' (1798) and 'Kubla Khan' (1816).

Tamsin Constable is a writer with an MA in Anthrozoology, specialising in human-wildlife connections and what nature means to people. She was section editor at *BBC Wildlife* magazine and now works for The Wild Network on how children, wild play and nature shape each other. @ConstableTL

Sue Croxford is a member of the Berkshire, Buckinghamshire and Oxfordshire Wildlife Trust and author of the Bug Mad Girl wildlife blog. The blog, which has been awarded *BBC Wildlife* magazine's blog of the week, can be found at www.bugmadgirl.blogspot.co.uk. Sue has also written magazine articles that have been published in *Best of British, Yours, Chiltern* and *Lymphoma Matters*.

Imtiaz Dharker is a Pakistan-born poet, artist and documentary filmmaker, whose many honours include the Queen's Gold Medal for Poetry. A fellow of the Royal Society of Literature, her work is featured on the UK's national curriculum, and discusses ideas of geographical and cultural displacement, conflict and gender politics. Her most recent poetry collection is *Over the Moon* (2014).

Jon Dunn is a natural history writer, photographer and wildlife tour leader based in the Shetland Isles. Author of *Britain's Sea Mammals*, his work takes him throughout Europe and the Americas. Once stalked by a mountain lion while birding on the edge of Mexico's notorious Sierra Madre Occidental, he generally prefers experiencing wildlife on his own terms and not as part of the food chain. www.jondunn.com

George Eliot was the pseudonym of Mary Ann Evans (d. 1880), a Victorian novelist whose *Middlemarch* (1871–2) was recently voted the greatest British novel of all time by a BBC poll of world critics and academics. Her other major works include *Adam Bede* (1859), *The Mill on the Floss* (1860) and *Silas Marner* (1861).

Thomas Furly Forster (d. 1825) was a botanist who compiled many lists and drawings of plants. After his death, his natural history journals were collated and published by his son as *The Pocket Encyclopaedia of Natural Phenomena*.

Alexi Francis is an artist and illustrator living in Sussex. All her life she has been a lover of wildlife and she studied zoology at university. She is interested in writing, especially about the natural world, and has had several articles published in anthologies and magazines such as *Earthlines*.

Elizabeth Gardiner (d. 2010) lived in a Wiltshire hamlet for over thirty years. She was a regular contributor to her local village broadsheet, her sparky 'Notes from Giddeahall' giving acute and witty insights into her neighbours, both human and animal, wild and domesticated, throughout the changing seasons. She was a prolific writer of short stories, articles and poetry, much of which remains unpublished.

Matt Gaw is a journalist who writes about experiences in nature close to his home in Suffolk. He contributes a monthly wildlife diary to the *Suffolk Magazine* and edits Suffolk Wildlife Trust's membership magazine. You can read his blog here: mattgawjournalist.wordpress.com

Sinéad Gleeson's essays have appeared in *Granta, Banshee* and *Winter Papers*. She is the editor of *The Long Gaze Back: An Anthology of Irish Women Writers* and *The Glass Shore: Short Stories by Women Writers from the North of Ireland*. She presents *The Book Show* on RTE Radio 1 and is currently working on a book of essays and a novel.

Caroline Greville is writing a book on her involvement with badgers in the context of her family life and wider rural setting. This memoir forms the main part of her PhD at the University of Kent, alongside research into new nature writing. She is Secretary of the East Kent Badger Group and teaches creative writing.

Thomas Hardy (d. 1928) wrote several famous works, including *Far from the Madding Crowd* (1874), *The Mayor of Casterbridge* (1886) and *Tess of the d'Urbervilles* (1891). Rural society was a major theme in his books; most were set in the partly imagined region of Wessex, based largely on areas of south and southwest England.

Will Harper-Penrose was brought up an outdoor child in the countryside of Cornwall. He has migrated to South London, as have the parakeets, where he writes about the city's rich and varied wildlife. In an ever-changing urban environment, he has no shortage of stories to tell about the animals that share his home. Will writes at wildsouthlondon.wordpress.com

Gerard Manley Hopkins (d. 1899) was a poet with a passion for writing descriptions of the natural world, with works including 'The Windhover' and 'The Sea and the Skylark'. He was also a priest and found himself conflicted between his religious belief and his poetry, giving the latter up for seven years at one point. Most of his poetry was not published during his lifetime.

Ted Hughes (d. 1998) was one of the twentieth century's most revered writers and poets, holding the position of Poet Laureate from 1984 until his death. Born and raised in rural Yorkshire, his work is permeated by a sense of natural wilderness, with animals a central theme. One of his most significant works is considered to be *Crow* (1970).

Alice Hunter is a wildlife and landscape photographer with a particular interest in European flora and butterflies and a passion for sharing her love of the natural world through her work. She loves being outdoors and writes regularly for several branches of The Wildlife Trusts as well as blogging about her experiences. Visit www.hunterphotos.co.uk to see Alice's work.

Richard Jefferies (d. 1887) was a nature writer of both essays and novels, inspired by his upbringing on a farm. His works include *The Amateur Poacher* (1879), *Round About a Great Estate* (1880), *Nature Near London* (1883) and *The Life of the Fields* (1884). The collection *Field and Hedgerow* was published posthumously in 1889.

Julian Jones's lifelong interest in eels began with slippery encounters alongside the Severn Estuary in the 1970s and culminated in a career with The Wildlife Trusts, conserving species and habitats, including wetlands that are home to this remarkable species. Julian's ambition is to help see the return of the burbot (also called eel pout) to Britain's waterways.

Patrick Kavanagh (d. 1967) is best known for his uncompromising portrayal of Irish country life, presenting a gritty reality that countered traditional pastoral romanticism. His best-known works include the novel *Tarry Flynn* (1948) based on his experiences as a young farmer, and the poems 'On Raglan Road' (1946) and 'The Great Hunger' (1942).

Dr Rob Lambert is an academic, broadcaster, birder and expedition ship lecturer, based at the University of Nottingham where he teaches and writes about environmental history, eco-tourism and nature–people relationships over time. He holds a Visiting Fellowship at the University of Western Australia, and is Vice-President of the Isles of Scilly Wildlife Trust. On 19 June 2015, Rob saw his 500th species of bird in the UK: a Cretzschmar's bunting on Bardsey Island.

Clare Leighton (d. 1989) was an artist, writer and illustrator famous for her work depicting scenes of rural life. Her best-known works include *The Farmer's Year: A Calendar of English Husbandry* (1933) and *Four Hedges: A Gardener's Chronicle* (1935).

John Lewis-Stempel's books include *The Wild Life: A Year of Living on Wild Food*, the *Sunday Times* top-ten bestseller *The Running Hare: The Secret Life of Farmland*, and *Meadowland*, the winner of the 2015 Thwaites Wainwright Prize for Nature Writing.

Amy Liptrot grew up on a sheep farm in Orkney, Scotland. She's a writer and her first book, *The Outrun*, a memoir, was published by Canongate in January 2016 and has been shortlisted for the Wellcome and Wainwright Book Prizes.

Helen Macdonald is a writer, naturalist and Cambridge University scholar who won widespread acclaim for her book *H is for Hawk* (2014), an account of training a goshawk following her father's death that was awarded the Samuel Johnson Prize and Costa Book Award, and was a *Sunday Times* bestseller.

Leanne Manchester works as Communications Officer for The Wildlife Trusts, coordinating the junior branch of the organisation: Wildlife Watch. She engages over 150,000 children and teenagers with nature every year through their quarterly magazine and inspiring projects. Her background in Biology led to volunteering and working for charities like the RSPCA and overseas conservation projects like Global Vision International.

Lucy McRobert is the Nature Matters campaigns manager for The Wildlife Trusts. She has written for publications including *BBC Wildlife*, is a columnist for *Birdwatch* magazine and was the Researcher on Tony Juniper's *What Nature Does for Britain* (2015). She is the creative director of A Focus On Nature, the youth nature network, and is a keen birdwatcher and mammal-watcher.

Matt Merritt, author of *A Sky Full Of Birds*, is the editor of *Bird Watching Magazine,* and a poet whose collections include *The Elephant Tests* (Nine Arches Press, 2013) and *hydrodaktulopsychicharmonica* (Nine Arches Press, 2010). He lives in Warwickshire and blogs at polyolbion.blogspot.co.uk

Chris Murphy, son of a Newry poulterer, grew up between Penny Lane and Strawberry Fields, crossing the Irish Sea in 1984 as a 'reverse migrant' and full-time nature conservationist with the RSPB. Now leading environmental campaigns and wildlife tours, he lives with his German wife, Doris, under the beam of St John's Point lighthouse on the Lecale Coast of County Down.

Benjamin Myers is an award-winning writer. His novels include *Turning Blue* (2016), *Beastings* (2014), *Pig Iron* (2012) and *Richard* (2010). He lives in the Upper Calder Valley, West Yorkshire. www.benmyers.com

Daphne Pleace has had previous lives in teaching, facilitation, and psychotherapy. She recently gained an MA in Creative Writing, and now specialises in nature writing and the links between nature and mental health and wellbeing. When not wandering the landscapes around her Devon home, or visiting wilder parts of Britain, she is working on her first book, and writes for conservation organisations.

Percy Bysshe Shelley (d. 1822) was a lyric and epic poet and progressive thinker of the Romantic era. His often radical views prevented his widespread acclaim until after his death. Today his works, including classics such as 'Ozymandias' (1818), are some of the best loved of the period, and have influenced figures from Oscar Wilde to Mahatma Gandhi.

Nan Shepherd (d. 1981) was a poet, novelist and English lecturer, whose work was fundamental in the advancement of early Scottish modernism. The local topography and climate, particularly of the Cairngorm Mountains, strongly influenced her poetry and writing, providing the backdrops for all three of her fictional works and for her much-loved non-fiction book *The Living Mountain* (1977).

Megan Shersby is a naturalist and keen moth-trapper living in Cambridgeshire. She is a committee member of A Focus On Nature, Britain's youth nature network. Her wildlife blog (mshersby.wordpress.com) came Highly Commended in the *BBC Wildlife* magazine's Wildlife Bloggers Award 2015, and she has also written for local Wildlife Trusts, the Moths Count project and the Mammals in a Sustainable Environment project.

Edward Step (d. 1931) was the author of numerous books on nature, both popular and specialist, including *Favourite Flowers of the Garden and Greenhouse* (1896), *The Romance of Wild Flowers* (1901), *Nature in the Garden* (1910) and *Nature Rambles: An Introduction to Country-lore* (1930).

Alfred, Lord Tennyson (d. 1892) remains one of Britain's most beloved poets.

Known for his lyrical and metrical mastery, his famous works include 'The Charge of the Light Brigade' (1854) and 'Crossing the Bar' (1889). He was the longest-serving Poet Laureate in history, and the first writer to be given peerage for his work, receiving a baronetcy from Queen Victoria.

Dylan Thomas (d. 1953) was a Welsh poet and writer. Although most famous for his poetry, including 'Do Not Go Gentle into That Good Night', his 'play for voices' *Under Milk Wood* is among his best-known works, having been adapted both for the stage and film.

Edward Thomas' (d. 1917) works were often noted for his portrayals of the English countryside, including *In Pursuit of Spring* (1914), *The Heart of England* (1906) and *The South Country* (1909).

Julia Wallis, now semi-retired, takes great pleasure in creative writing. Although poetry calls loudest, she is also drawn to nature writing and has her first novel under way. Living on the edge of the countryside and helping out on a Midlands smallholding, she is never short of inspiration. Writing jostles for time alongside beekeeping, spinning and a plethora of country crafts.

Reverend Gilbert White (d. 1793) was a curate, as well as a keen naturalist and ornithologist. His best known work is *The Natural History and Antiquities of Selborne* (1789); his journals were published posthumously, in 1931. He is considered by many to have been a major influence in forming modern attitudes to and respect for nature.

Janet Willoner lives in North Yorkshire and has been passionate about nature since childhood. She studied and taught Natural Sciences, had a career as a landscape watercolourist and took up writing on retirement. She has always loved spending time in wild places, experiencing solitude and observing wildlife, all of which inspire her art and writing.

Woolhope Naturalists' Field Club was founded in 1851 as a society dedicated to the study of Herefordshire's natural history, geology and archaeology. Prestigious members have included Edward Elgar, Roderick Murchison and the botanist George Bentham. Early members' interest in fungi led to the formation of the British Mycological Society.

Annie Worsley is a mother of four and grandmother living on a coastal croft in the remote Northwest Highlands of Scotland. A former academic who explored the relationships between humans and environments in diverse parts of the world, including Papua New Guinea, she now writes about nature, wildlife and landscape. She tries to paint the wild using words.

William Butler Yeats (d. 1939) was a leading figure of British and Irish twentieth-century literary society, and one of the greatest poets of his time. *The Tower* (1928) is often considered his best poetic offering, with recurring themes including Irish nationalism, folklore, mysticism and the occult. He was the first Irishman to be awarded the Nobel Prize in Literature.